MOMENTS LIKE THIS

SYLVIA SILVETTI HAVLISH

MOMENTS LIKE THIS
SYLVIA SILVETTI HAVLISH

Published by:

Joshua Tree Publishing

www.JoshuaTreePublishing.com

ISBN: 0-9829803-8-8
13-Digit: 978-0-9829803-8-5

Printed in the United States of America

Author Websites: SylviaHavlish.com
MoreMomentsLikeThis.com

Front Cover Image © Regor Imperator

DEDICATION

To

DOROTHY POWELL
AND
TASHA POWELL

TWO ANGELS SENT TO ME BY GOD
TO OPEN THE PATH TO THIS BOOK!

I AM FOREVER GRATEFUL
FOR YOUR BELIEF AND ENCOURAGEMENT!

TABLE OF CONTENTS

A Note from the Author

Sylvia Silvetti Havlish

It was the end of another full day of work, and I was driving home from my office about ten p.m. The red light seemed so long at that particular corner as the wind and rain were growing stronger. I waited impatiently to see the green signal. I sensed a very emphatic thought or voice inside of me: *You're going home and write a story called Eleven Days.*

I closed my eyes and shook my head slightly as if to come back to reality. But the voice was stronger, more urgent…repeating the same message. I thought to myself, *Sylvia, you've got to clear your head, something is wrong.* But for the third time, I heard the message.

The light changed. I turned towards home. My thoughts were racing. *Eleven Days? What in the world is that?*

I arrived home, went right to the computer, and started typing. It was as if someone else was doing the writing. I had never experienced anything ever like this! I typed the first two sentences…then went to the unpacked box from my mom's room that I had yet to put away after her death. On top was a large calendar from the month of September, 2003. The hospice nurse had hung the calendar on the wall across from my mom's hospital bed in the room at home at my mother's request. She had started to "X" out the days on the first day my mother came home from the hospital. I quickly counted the "X's"…oh my! She lived eleven days from the first day she came back home until the day she passed away.

I had never been aware of that fact until that night. I returned to the keyboard, and the story just "flowed out" of my hands. It was like nothing I had ever experienced in my life. When I was finished, I ran to my husband. I must have looked like a "wild woman"...my coat still on, my face covered with tears, and a "manuscript" in my hand. I read it to him through tears and sobs. He was stunned. He was crying, too. I tried to explain to him what had occurred in my car and that this was the result. We stared at each other in silence and both knew that something amazing had just happened.

"What will you do with this?" he asked.

"I have no idea," I answered, "...probably just keep it and show it to my brother. It is good therapy."

In retrospect, it is now clear to me, beyond a shadow of a doubt, that God was preparing me for the book you are now holding. I have had many dreams in my life and have tried to go "confidently in the direction" of some of those dreams. But to have a book published? That was not even near the top of my list...or perhaps was never even on the list!

All this happened in the year 2004...and I know now that God was whispering many ideas and thoughts in my head as these last eight years have passed. I remember thinking one night that "... if I ever did have a book, it would be named after my dad's song, *Moments Like This*.

When I had the confidence to start sharing my story, *Eleven Days*, with my bereavement groups, many of the clients would tell me that it should be published; so many asked me for copies of my story.

I have always taught my clients to write for good therapy as I had done for so many years. I merely sat at the computer when I was sad, lonely, upset or angry, and poured out my heart. And just as it did on that night in the storm, these stories have "flowed" from my heart... and from the hearts of my many clients, family members, and friends.

Thank you, God.

Sylvia Silvetti Havlish

February, 2012

WE LOSE OUR PARENTS

We are taught that it is the way of life to expect that we will all lose our parents. Then our minds take over into the great "denial" zone, and we decide that our parents will be very, very old when it is time for them to die. We believe that we have a long time until we will have to deal with that. But life doesn't always "wait" for them to be old…and for us, their children, to be ready. No matter our ages when our parents pass away, or their ages, we may suddenly feel a terrible abandonment…and we feel we are orphans.

So much of our response to losing our parents depends on the relationship we had with them during our lives. The stories in this section of Moments Like This reflect the profound differences of our grieving based on the past relationships we lived. When I share some of my experiences as a daughter with my friends and clients, I am always reminded of how "lucky" I was to have had the type of parents I had. My brother, Mike, wrote a wonderful song about our childhood days aptly called, How Lucky We Were. Somehow I don't think of it as "luck" but as one of the greatest blessings I have been given. I believe that the greatest tribute I can pay to my parents is to pray that somehow my son will see my parents in me.

As Wayne Dyer teaches in his book, Gifts from Eykis, it is never too late to have a happy childhood! Grieving our parents is a time of reflection. Learn from your memories, then learn to forgive and move on.

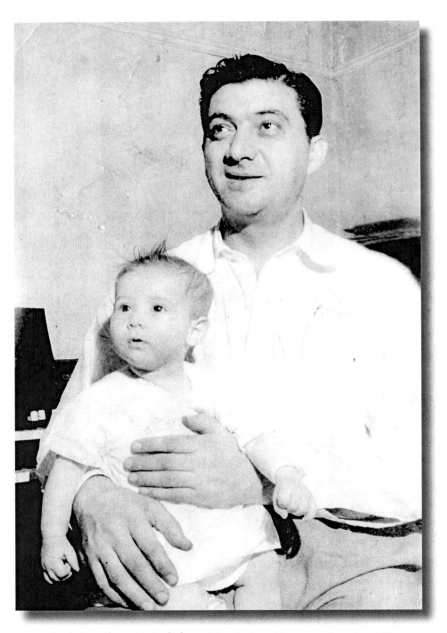

Sylvia Silvetti Havlish and her father, Samuel Silvetti, 1948.

MOMENTS LIKE THIS...WITH SAM
Sylvia Silvetti Havlish

H e told me once that the happiest day in his life was when he held his little girl on his lap on the bench of his new Hammond organ. The picture I see from my computer is that very day...saved forever in black and white. He looks ecstatic; I look safe, secure and completely where I was supposed to be! And those feelings became stronger as I grew up! That picture signifies the beginning of a wonderful father/daughter relationship that continued until the day I watched my father's soul leave his body.

He was a gifted musician and a handsome, witty and loving Italian father. My brother, Mike, along with my mom and our dog, Skippy, made up the rest of the family. We had a childhood filled with his beautiful music and rolling laughter. It was the best of times.

It never occurred to me that we might not have enough money because the love, good food and great music that we lived with each day filled all the spaces of our lives. I remember the car trips to New York City as we set off to go to museums and window shop with my mother while "Sam" went to the music publishers to have his songs reviewed. He never let on to us whether he had a good reception or not. I remember reaching up for his hand and marveling at the fact that I was with the best looking man in New York City! At the time, I thought all children had trips to NYC and met all these interesting people along the way.

My moments alone with my father are among the best memories of my life. While I attended a local college just fifteen miles from home, he would arrive on two Wednesday afternoons a month to take me to lunch. He played piano and organ (together at the same time!) in a fine dining restaurant in another city and had to leave our home each day at 5:30 p.m. So on those Wednesday afternoons, he was always dressed in a beautiful suit, white-starched shirt, and handsome tie ready to entertain the diners that evening with his beautiful melodies. I remember some of the students asking me who the "handsome older man" was that I met on those special days!

Samuel Silvetti, 1953.

It was during those wonderful lunch dates that we talked together. Some of the most important philosophies in my life came from those conversations. Most of the best lessons I absorbed about life, spirituality, and politics came from those talks. Oh, how I miss those times!

He used to tell beautiful stories of his beloved parents when they came to America from Abruzzi, Italy. There were many children, but his mother seemed to have a very special place in her heart for "Sammy." When he was sixteen years old, his mother died from a massive stroke. He never got to say goodbye to her, but always spoke of her in glowing, adoring terms. I always felt so sad that I never knew my grandparents as they both died before I was born. And so this brings me to the story of his death.

He was just seventy-one years young. He had a lifetime of smoking cigarettes as most musicians did then…but he had quit smoking five years prior when he needed five bypasses in his heart. We all felt that perhaps we could rest easy when we were told that the cigarettes caused his heart to "break" but that he had somehow beat lung cancer. We were wrong.

In early August of 1985, he found a lump on his neck. After the biopsy, I was with him when he went in to the doctor to get the results. The doctor couldn't even look at us as he explained that "…it's cancer, Sam, and it's already everywhere…" I felt like someone hit me in the stomach with a baseball bat. My dad stood up quickly, turned on his heel, and said, "Let's get the hell out of here." And with that, his denial began…and my terror took hold. As my dad quickly walked out of the office, the doctor grabbed my arm and whispered to me that he might have a few months. I was hit in the stomach again.

All I remember about driving him home is that it was the only car ride we ever had in total silence. I was fighting back tears and assumed he was trying to digest this new information. He got out of the car and said he was taking a nap. I was left to tell my mom and brother. I was thirty-six years old, but at that moment, I just wanted to grab my daddy's hand and take a walk in New York City as if nothing had happened in between.

That was August 3. By October, I had taken a leave from my job as a high school counselor when I told them I would be back when my dad went "home." I just couldn't handle the stress of driving between my town and his…and worrying sick the rest of the time. I spent October with my precious parents going to radiation treatments, welcoming relatives and friends as they came to visit, and listening to my dad play his beautiful piano. The last time he played for me, his choice of songs told us the real story: *Pennies from Heaven, Smile, I'll be Seeing You*, and *Somewhere over the Rainbow*. I have a tape recording of that "concert" in our living room, and when I listen to it even 26 years later, tears stream down my face.

On Monday, November 4th, he lapsed into a "coma" at noon. The doctor came and told us that he was displaying every sign that this would be the day he went to God. At 7:15 that evening, my mom and I went in the bedroom to move him a little to avoid any bed sores. Just as we were on each side of his bed, his eyes suddenly opened wide…he tried to sit up…and as he looked right past us, he called, "Mama!" The tone of his voice and the inflection of this word told us that she had come to welcome him to Heaven. After all those years, his beloved mother had come for him.

At that, he slowly lay back down as all the pain, anguish, and struggling left his face and body. He took his last breath as the "peace that passes all understanding" swept across his beautiful face.

We didn't cry. My brother had come in with his son…and we all just stood in silence trying to drink in the peace and awesome power that filled that room. None of us could see my grandmother, but there was no denying that my precious father entered his Heavenly home on the arm of his mother.

We had kept the tape player going almost constantly while he was sick so he could listen to his own music and the music of his favorite musicians. I realized that just as he was taking his final few breaths, *Moments Like This* started playing on the recorder.

As we all stood together at his bedside, I could hear the incredibly beautiful and appropriate words of his song:

Soft winds that blow, two hearts aglow, stars shining above...
Moments like this cannot be denied me, summer is here, I'm in love!
Soft melodies, weird harmonies sound far in the night...
With you in my arms your two lips to kiss and more of moments like this.
Though years will go by, we will grow old, our love will never die.
For sweet memories weave through the years
Treasures of moments like this!
Stars growing dim, dawn lights the sky, time now for a dream...
So kiss me again while I make a wish for more...
More moments like this!

Dream on, my sweet Daddy.

Love, Sylvia

Sylvia Silvetti Havlish and her mom, Lena Silvetti, 1953.

ELEVEN DAYS
Sylvia Silvetti Havlish

I t was mid-September…always her favorite time of the year. In my imagination, I could hear her repeating her favorite poem in her "sing-song" beautiful voice of my childhood memory. "The goldenrod is yellow…the corn is turning brown…the trees in apple orchards, with fruit are bending down. The gentian's bluest fringes are curling in the sun…in dusty pods the milkweed…its hidden silk has spun. By all these lovely tokens, September days are here with summer's best of weather and autumn's best of cheer!"*

But today she wasn't singing…although her beautiful smile still lit up the room when the young oncologist entered her hospital room. She had been there for six weeks after her diagnosis of uterine cancer. During the surgery he found that her cancer was in stage four…and had spread "everywhere." She was 90. She was 90 going on 35…and I couldn't bear to hear his next words.

"Lena, we've done all that we can do medically for you. It's time to make a decision about further chemotherapy."

"I've made my decision," she quickly answered. "I'm not having any more chemo. I'm ready. My body is broken, and I'm ready. And anyway, my husband was here earlier, and he's waiting for me."

My dad had passed away from lung cancer eighteen years earlier, but she had told me that she had seen him sitting in the chair in the corner just waiting to welcome her home. There was no mistaking the honesty and love with which she spoke. Her love for my dad…

although she felt hurt many times in their marriage…and her love for this young doctor, who had tried so valiantly to save this magical woman of love and light, was obvious. She was actually trying to make this easier for him! And wasn't that just like my Lena!

"Well, then, Lena, I'll make arrangements for you to move down one floor to the Hospice unit…or you could choose to go home." Then I blurted out, "She's coming home!"

"Yes," she said, "I want to go home."

It was my home, which we had been blessed to share with her for the past 12 years…my husband, my son, and me. We were a family of four, and she was definitely the "center," the "core," the strength. I knew that we just couldn't allow her to die in a hospital no matter how lovely they made the surroundings.

He explained to us that since it was late afternoon, an ambulance would not be available to take her to our home until the next day, and so in an hour, the nurses would move her from the "Transitional Care Unit" to the Hospice unit below.

I watched the doctor cry openly as he bent down to hug my sweet mother…and she comforted him and thanked him for giving her his "best shot"…as she called it! He whispered, "Lena, I'll see you again in Heaven." Now I was sobbing and went out into the hall to try and collect myself.

Then I witnessed the entire staff of the "TSU"…nurses, aides, nutritionists, and janitors…all file in to say their good byes to this lovely, sweet woman who had been the best mother any family could be lucky enough to have! There were more tears, even some laughter… with her wit so sharp and quick…it was her pleasure to make other people smile and laugh! We gathered up her possessions…her many flowers and gifts…and I walked slowly behind her bed as they pushed her to her temporary home downstairs.

As I tucked her in for the night and offered to stay with her, she "sent me home" to rest and to get ready for her return to Brookside Road the next day. She told me to call my brother, Mike, and have him come down for the trip home. He lived about sixty-five miles north and had been traveling the highway for the six weeks since surgery. We had a few "false alarms" when the staff thought sure she was "passing," but she always rallied...and now I was certain she would rally again.

As I entered the Hospice wing the next morning, I was struck with the beautiful, comfortable, and inviting surroundings. The nurses were among the most sensitive professionals we had encountered on this journey through the valley of the shadow of death. I thought of them as "midwives of death"...as they helped to prepare the patient and the family members for this last "parade."

Then I entered her room to see our Lutheran Pastor, who had just started his tenure at our church about six months before my mother fell ill, bending over her bed praying for her deliverance into heaven. They said the Lord's Prayer together as I watched quietly from the doorway. He patted her hands and then also told her that he would see her in Heaven. I was picturing the crowd that she would have there already...and wondering where in the world this doctor and this pastor would fit in!

As he left, he gave me that look that said, "I know you're smiling on the outside, Sylvia, but crying on the inside." He was right. But what my mom said next was not what I expected.

She was almost sitting up...with many pillows holding her up in bed...with a wide smile on her face...and this incredible look of a woman who knows what she's doing and where she's going. She was a woman on a mission!

"Listen," she said as she pulled me closer to whisper in my ear, "do you still have that friend who is a Catholic priest?"

"You mean 'Bubba'?" I asked.

"Yes, Linda's brother! Is he a priest?"

"Yes, mom, he's a college chaplain just a few miles away."

"Good," she said, "call him! Ask him if he will come to give the *Last Rites*."

You see my dad was Italian and Catholic when they met...and she was a divorced Lutheran with a child from her first marriage.

Her German family decided she was the "black sheep" of the family for going with a "musician who plays in saloons"...and his Italian Catholic family was absolutely beside themselves that he would stoop to marry a Protestant woman with a ready-made family! But my brother Mike and I...the two kids born to the two black sheep...were the lucky ones. We got the best two people in both families...barring none!

So, in the beginning of our lives, we were baptized in the Catholic church, even though my parents were considered pariahs. We attended church with my Aunt Rose...the saintly church organist... until my dad declared when I was four years old that we would be joining the Lutheran Church so we could all go as a family.

WOW! Now we were all pariahs!!! Or was it Lutheran??? But we attended as a family and found out that the same God who resided at St. Joseph's Roman Catholic Church had found His way over to Holy Trinity Lutheran Church! As a five-year-old, I thought the only difference was that Lutherans spoke English, and Catholics spoke Latin! It seemed to me that with a few exceptions, our "mass" (service) on Sunday was almost word-for-word the same as in the other church, but in English!!

But here we were...my Protestant mother and me, the Catholic Protestant daughter...calling "Father Bubba" as he was lovingly called by friends...to come and administer the "service of the sick." It seemed like he was there in no time at all. How thankful I am for his treatment of us that day. There was never a question from him when my sweet Lutheran mother pulled out her rosary beads...my dad's beads from childhood...that she had been secretly praying with for years...and the three of us recited the Rosary and the Lord's Prayer in unison. I think he must still be wondering how the Lutherans present that morning knew all the words perfectly!

So now, Father Bubba was leaving and again, saying that he would see her in Heaven. It was really getting crowded now. And when he exited her room, she looked up at me with those sparkling blue eyes and with a twinkle in her eyes and mischief in her face asked me if I knew any rabbis! We both laughed and hugged—and then I cried silently. I kept thanking God for this amazing woman who was actually preparing to leave this earth with a big smile of confidence! For as my former Pastor said later when I told him this story, "She wasn't taking any chances. She was covering all her religious bases." I can see her now "sliding into home plate," having hit every base…the Catholics, the Protestants, and the Jews! That would be Lena.

The arrangements were made for an ambulance to bring her to our home, and we arranged for a hospital bed to be put in my bedroom so that I could be near her for as long as she would stay.

In that regard, her hospice nurse asked me to come out in the hall as the ambulance crew was preparing her bed for transport. She held my hand and gently explained to me that in "their experience," one of two things would happen this evening. She would come home and then quietly "slip away" knowing the peace of her own home *or*, she would have a "rally" and stay for as long as her body would hold out. I was voting for the second one…and I got my wish!

She stayed with us for eleven more days.

And for the first ten of those eleven days, she was bright, smiling, singing, and peaceful…although in pain…but she never complained once about her own condition. I got to see "the peace that passes all understanding." She was living it. I knew that her epitaph should read: "Death came and found her living!"

Music had always been one of the greatest blessings in our family. My father was a gifted pianist, organist, songwriter, and wonderful, fun-loving dad. My mother sang and hummed along as he was playing his beautiful music. I can still go back to those moments in my mind whenever I want to hear this again. My brother, Mike, was the one to inherit my father's special talent. He is a songwriter, singer, pianist, and guitarist in his own right…and he is wonderful! So, we kept playing my dad's tapes and my brother's tapes…along with her favorite singer, Nat King Cole. The beautiful music filled her room, and she kept singing along and smiling for ten days. She was beautiful, inside and out.

Sylvia Silvetti Havlish and her mom, Lena Silvetti

'The nurses who came to help us were mesmerized by her wonderful memory for all the words to the music my dad and my brother were "playing" on the tapes. She loved to tell stories...and she had thousands of them...and these women loved to hear them. The friends and family members who were visiting and ministering to her would all say the same thing to me as they left. "She's amazing! She's so positive, so cheery, so gracious."

Yes, that would be my Lena.

It was day ten, and her only two living sisters came to visit for the last time. Aunt Evelyn was at least five or six years older than my mom...and Aunt Helen was the "baby" at eighty-five. They were both fighting back tears as she just smiled and tried to soothe *them*! But, I could tell that she was tired and that her happy blue eyes just couldn't stay opened as long as they had that morning.

And then, my brother and his son's family (two great-grandchildren) said their last good byes. She was really tired then. It was Saturday night, and they had to drive back to Berwick...and she just couldn't keep her eyes open. I knew that it was the last time they would talk with her. I could barely walk them to the front door, and we all choked back tears as we waved goodbye. My brother wanted to stay, but she wouldn't hear of it. After all, he had a "gig" the next day for an evening party at the country club. And as she knew so well from being married to my dad, they never backed out on any performance. She just wouldn't have it. She told him to "go and play one for me!" I knew by her unspoken message that I was not to call him until she was "home."

When everyone had finally gone, I kissed her goodnight, held her as close to me as I could, and then she whispered, "Don't worry honey, I'll still be here in the morning." And she was.

I thought perhaps she was going to rally again on day eleven… September 28, 2003…and I asked her if I could give her something to eat. She was eating applesauce and pudding for the past seven days. She nodded that she would eat so she could take her medicine. Of course, my mind went into overdrive hoping that she would have a miraculous burst of wellness from these medicines so I could keep her for years and years.

She did manage to allow me to give her two bites of the pudding and then pushed my hand away and shook her head. "No more," she whispered, "I want to rest."

In about an hour, it all started. All the physical clues that her body was getting ready to stop. Our closest friends started pouring in about two p.m. She could barely speak now but found a way to lovingly hold the hands of my son, Chris…and his beautiful girlfriend, Laura . The last thing I remember her saying aloud was to Laura: "Take good care of my grandson!"

We formed a circle around her bed…as my dad's beautiful melodies played on the tape machine…and we sang her favorite hymns and her favorite songs. We all kept talking to her, although she looked as if she was sleeping fitfully. She started "struggling" late in the afternoon, and her breathing became labored and difficult. The hospice nurse was on the phone with me instructing me to keep administering the oral morphine that they had trained me to use.

I knew that she needed to hear me say that it was okay to go now...to find my dad and find God and follow the light. I could no longer stand to see her struggling to breathe, so I whispered to her that we would all be okay and that we were ready for her to go. The nurse on the phone kept assuring me that the morphine I was giving her was helping her.

Why did it not seem like that was true? The next several hours were the worst in my life. I started pleading with her to let go... to sleep in God's arms...but it seemed like she was just unable to let it all go. It's the first question I'm going to ask her when I break in to the crowded room in heaven when I get there: "Where were you, sweet mommy, during that time??? Please tell me that I wasn't prolonging your agony with that damned medicine...please take my guilt away." I will never allow my son to be the one who has to "see me out" at the end if I have a vote. I wouldn't change anything about caring for her except those last hours. I know that she wouldn't want me going crazy with guilt about whether or not I was helping her but I have so many unanswered questions.

However, at exactly 10:30 p.m. on Sunday night, September 28, 2003, the angels finally carried the beautiful soul of Lena Smith Silvetti to her heavenly home. She told me several days before that the first thing she was going to do was dance with my father!

I can see them now...in their 30s...slim, beautiful, full of life... dancing and smiling and holding each other as he twirls her around the dance floor of heaven. And as they dance, she is saying, "The goldenrod is yellow, the corn is turning brown...the trees in apple orchards, with fruit are bending down!"

Sylvia Silvetti Havlish
October 17, 2006

*Quote from the Poem "September" by Helen Hunt Jackson 1830-85

MOMENTS WITH MY DAD
Michael Berney

Richard Berney, my father, was the rarest of men: a male who radiated a spiritual quality and love for others. Friend to all who knew him, he brought out the best in people. Dad set me free to define my own goals in life, inspired me to believe in my abilities, and then stepped aside and rejoiced.

He was a wonderful man, and a devoted dad. For instance, I still remember as a little kid going out in the back yard with him, asking him to hit me baseballs from dinner 'til dark. It's one of my earliest memories and one of the fondest. He used to get such a kick out of hitting those ground balls, coaching me how to go left, go right, stay in front of the ball, get my glove down...in a word, fundamentals. And he drilled them into me with discipline and patience...characteristics I proudly model today.

He and I could talk about every subject: politics and current events, mathematics and science, sports and card games. He might not let me play poker with him, but he let me watch. In the 1950s, he particularly enjoyed the Friday night Berney-family poker game, which continues to this day. He let me watch his bridge foursome play in our basement every week, from the time I was ten, and he let me play bridge as his partner in my first tournament at age sixteen. We talked about weightier topics too: religion, philosophy, psychology and the meaning of life. We talked about "things" and about "feelings;" about anything...and he was a great listener!

Dad's life was built on love. He adored "his" Louise. It had been "love at first sight" and they were engaged in 1927, at age eighteen. They were engaged for eight years...he wouldn't marry her until he could support her without her parents' money...he was fiercely independent. They were married for forty-two more years until in 1977, he passed. The day he passed, in his own bed in his humble home, she was by his side, as they had been together all those years.

My first son, Chris, was also born in 1977, and I recall thinking about "The Great Mandela" the Wheel of Life, a song sung by Peter, Paul and Mary. Life begins, life ends. Later I would tell Chris and his brother Scott "Grandpop stories" because they had never known this extraordinary man who was their grandfather.

He was very ill by March 1977, when Chris was born. But I remember vividly the day in 1973 when his illness first became real. He was seemingly in good health, and he and I were out for a walk. I noticed a little lump on his neck as we were walking through the neighborhood in Baltimore. It was a cool crisp spring day, a day when it felt great to be alive. As we walked along the boulevard, I saw the lump and asked what it was. He didn't know, and for once, he didn't want to talk about it. He said it would probably go away soon, and we resumed talking. My goodness, we talked about everything on that walk...big things, little things, everything and nothing...same as always. Life was good. When we got back home, I asked him to get the lump checked out. He reluctantly agreed.

Dad had been a smoker for years in his youth; it was the cool thing to do in his day. Somewhere in midlife, he decided to quit, and he did it "cold turkey." He had iron-willed self-discipline. But now, decades after quitting, the cigarettes like a jilted lover had decided to pay him back.

It was a malignant tumor, spread through lymph nodes from his nasal pharynx to other spots. In 1973 that was a death sentence for most folks. But Dad was a fighter and wouldn't go quietly. Maybe his quick response after the walk gave him four more years. He fought for every day of those four years, winning a few battles, losing most, but continuing to offer cheerful counsel to one and to all who stopped to see him.

Less than ten days before he died, I stopped by to see him. He seemed in particularly good spirits that day, and I needed help solving a business problem. I decided to ask his advice, despite his frail condition.

Often, he and I would go back and forth, challenging each other and testing our viewpoints by bouncing them off each other. Today, as it turned out, that wasn't necessary.

"I need an analyst for my staff," I said. "Given a choice between hiring a guy in his thirties with some experience, who is very capable, but somewhat more abrasive and perhaps more difficult to supervise, or hiring a twenty-two-year-old guy with no experience, excellent potential and extremely personable, who would you hire, Dad?" It seemed like a complex decision to me. I was twenty-nine at the time.

"Will the abrasive person be able to persuade others of his viewpoint?" Dad asked. With that simple question my dilemma was solved!

The clear answer was "no" and Dad didn't have to say another word. Good thing, too, because he probably couldn't have said much more in his condition. Yet in that one shining albeit frail moment, a moment that somehow came out of the past and lit up the present like a beacon, he did what he always did best: he let me *help myself to find the right answer.*

I was there for part of that day with Dad, but I drove from Baltimore back to Central Pennsylvania, back to work, knowing exactly what I wanted to do, not because he told me the answer, but because he showed me how it would reveal itself to me if I just let it.

As the twilight of his days quickly turned to darkness, he reminded me of some of the simple foundations of a life well-lived, of his world: creativity, the skill to bring order from chaos, discipline, the Socratic knack of teaching by questioning and if necessary jousting a bit, and above all, patience and love. Today, and for all the 35 years since his passing, these have been the foundation of my life with my wife, Beth, our sons, our granddaughters and their beautiful families. I watch with pride and joy as my sons apply these same lessons I applied, learned from moments with my Dad.

Michael Berney
2012

GRATEFUL HEARTS
Linda Permar, RN

In my lifetime, I have been blessed with not only a wonderful family, but also with extraordinary friends. It has been my pleasure to have known Linda Permar for many years…meeting her first as an "adult student" in a class I taught called "The Beautiful You." It was a class I designed to blend my knowledge of "inner beauty" from my counseling background with the facts about skin care and glamour I learned as a Sales Director for Mary Kay Cosmetics. It was designed to be a fun, six-night course on being beautiful from the "inside, out."

Linda was one person who really stood out in my class with her lovely demeanor and her beautiful heart. Linda was a nurse in the "well-baby" nursery at our local hospital, and we instantly started a friendship that has grown and blossomed. One of the most incredible parts of our "friendship journey" has been that we were both daughters who loved our parents…cared for them…and then lost them in an eerily close proximity of time. Over the years we have often compared our journeys of grief over many cups of tea.

When I told Linda that I was putting together a book about the "moments" in our lives, she immediately agreed to write her memories of her journey of grief with her sweet parents. Her stories follow.

Sylvia Silvetti Havlish

MY DAD
Linda Permar, RN

My dad, Kenneth died on September 13, 1985. He was diagnosed with ALS in 1982. I travelled every four months to Iowa from my home in Pennsylvania arranging help for my mother and father during his illness. Mom got her driver's license for the very first time at age 62 when Dad couldn't drive any longer. Hospice became very important to us during this time. George and Elsie from the Hospice program were great supports to my parents.

My dad had been a milkman and was a talkative, social man who loved people. Since my dad was such a "talker" and so loved to communicate, losing his ability to speak so others could understand him was devastating to him. We made an alphabet board, and he used a wooden dowel between his teeth to point out the letters to us. He had lost all use of his arms and hands early in the disease. It seemed that his illness progressed very quickly, and he needed much help with daily activities.

Each visit was a new challenge to help him and my family to cope. Dad became frustrated easily with the slow process it took to let us know what he needed. My brother, Mark, came to live with my parents at this time to help out. Dad appreciated the help but wanted to do more himself.

It was very difficult for him to express his feelings, but he would say how grateful he was for the help. On one visit, I taught Mom and my brother and sister how to "suction" Dad's breathing tube. His muscles were weak including those for respirations and fluid would build up. Soon Dad could not eat solid food as there was danger of "aspiration" and pneumonia could set it. Dad needed a feeding tube. The medical personnel put a feeding tube in with much difficulty due to his poor gag reflex. When the time came for the feeding tube to be changed, I knew that he would not tolerate it. After much pleading, the neurologist finally agreed to a gastric feeding tube directly into his stomach. Dad needed nutrition.

He travelled 100 miles to the VA Hospital for the surgery. On September 4 he celebrated his sixty-third birthday. I sent him balloons and a long letter. He did fine after the surgery. About one day or so before he died, he asked mom to go home. She had been staying in an apartment across from the hospital with George and Elsie from Hospice. The pastor visited and prayed with him.

Just before they were going to try and feed him liquid food through the gastric tube, he died. I feel he was trying to spare my mother all the difficulties that would ensue. He knew his time to be with God was coming soon.

My mother joined him 18 years later to the very day to be with God in peace.

~

My mother, Frances, died September 13, 2003. In 2001, my mother had a massive stroke with left-side paralysis, impaired speech, and cognitive limitations. My sister and I both took family leaves and spent sixty-three days with her throughout extensive rehabilitation. Given her determination and hard work, she did very well in rehabilitation.

She so enjoyed seeing "her girls" every day. We liked to think of ourselves as her "other rehab team," giving her much love and encouragement. Because of this tragedy with our mom, my sister and I became much closer. Our mom qualified for a special rehab center that specialized in brain injury after her stay at the hospital rehab. She was very lucky to obtain a spot in this facility and improved so much. However, it was not enough improvement for her to return to her apartment. It was determined that her cognitive skills were not developed enough for her to remain safely on her own, although my sister lived nearby.

We began looking for skilled nursing facilities. After much searching, we decided on one in our hometown. I thought of taking her to Pennsylvania where I live but I knew that her friends and the majority of her family were in Iowa. Mom's happiness was most important to me.

I travelled to Iowa as often as I could to see my mother. During these visits we would go out to lunch or just go for a drive and get ice cream. Mom loved our times together and so did I. We would sit on the porch of the facility and just talk.

She loved her friend, Emma, who was 110 years young at the time. Emma was the oldest living Iowan, and together they tended the flowers on the porch. We often attended a Bible study and played games with the other residents. I cherish the memories of those wonderful times with my mom. Since being married and moving to Pennsylvania, I had only seen my mother on an average of once a year.

The day mom died two years later, she remarked to me during our phone conversation that she wasn't feeling well. My sister, niece and family along with my youngest brother had been visiting her that day. They had brought a specialty sandwich from our hometown that was mom's favorite. Later my sister told me that she had found mom sitting alone in her wheelchair just staring out the window as the rain came down. Mom told her she was thinking about Dad. Eighteen years prior, on this very day, my Dad had died. Later in the evening of that day, I called to talk with Mom again to see how she was feeling. Her voice sounded weak, and she said she wasn't feeling any better.

It was about eight p.m. and she was tired and wanted to go to bed. As I often had done in the past, I called the nurses' station to have someone check on her and to make her comfortable in bed. Mom was not a person to continue to ask for help. She said she knew they would come when they could. Everyone loved my sweet mother.

Later that evening, about ten p.m. my mother died in her nurse's arms after complaining of back pain. My parents died on the very same day, September 13th, exactly eighteen years apart.

Linda Permar, RN

Postscript from Sylvia:

As Linda and I talked over the years, we realized that both of our parents had died in the fall...eighteen years apart!

My father, Sam Silvetti, died on November 4, 1985...Linda's dad on September 13, 1985. Eighteen years later, my mother, Lena Silvetti, passed into the arms of God on September 28th, 2003. Linda's sweet mother left on September 13th, 2003.

We often say that we are now "orphans" and that since we both live "away" from the rest of our families...that we are so blessed that we have each other. We truly celebrate our friendship...and we feel a love and camaraderie that is very special indeed. I picture our four parents, meeting up in heaven, and discussing their two daughters! I'm sure they laugh right along with us as we recount our many memories! God bless you, Linda, my friend.

Sylvia Silvetti Havlish
2012

Remembering Mom
Laura Smith Lance

My mom, Pat Smith, retired from teaching around three in the afternoon on Friday, June 6, 2008 at sixty years of age. Never did I imagine that twenty hours later my father and I would be sitting in a funeral home trying to come to terms with a startling and painful new reality that mom was no longer with us.

Around 10:30 p.m. that Friday night, I walked into our house in West Virginia to discover Mom, lying face down on the floor in the house. What happened next was a blur of screams, frantic efforts by my boyfriend and father to resuscitate her, 911 calls, and a parade of emergency responders, neighbors and friends. I just sat paralyzed in another room, because I knew the moment I saw her that she was gone. I was twenty-four years old, and my mom was gone.

To say that her heart attack was unexpected would be a lie. If I was honest with myself, I had been expecting this eventually for years as Mom had struggled with Type 2 Diabetes and weight issues for many, many years. However, expecting and experiencing are two totally different things. Over the next day or so, family and friends filtered in from across the country, mom's former and current students brought us food and sent cards, and people we had not heard from in ages came out of the woodwork to support us.

Deep down I was struggling with a great deal of guilt and anger. My guilt was over two main issues: 1) Mom died alone, which is something I believe no one should have to endure. 2) My last words to her were a rushed, "I'm running late. I don't have time to deal with this now. We will talk about it later." There would be no later, and my mom deserved better than that as the last words from her only child. I was angry that Mom had just retired and would not get to enjoy the fruits of her labor and the relaxation for which she had waited so long. Her death did not seem fair, but then again to the grieving family, death rarely seems fair. I was also angry at Mom. Angry that she had not taken better care of herself. Angry that she had left Dad and me alone. And angry as I watched my normally rock solid Dad crumble right before my eyes.

On the flip side, I was also grateful. You see, if it had been a normal Friday evening, I would not have been in Wheeling, West Virginia, for a friend's wedding. I would have been sitting in my home in Atlanta, Georgia. I don't even want to think about how hard it would have been for Dad to make that phone call and for me to travel home for my Mom's funeral. In a turn of fate, I had been laid off of my job in Atlanta the week prior and had decided that instead of coming home for the weekend, I would spend the entire week at home. This allowed me to spend more time with Mom in her last week than I had been able to spend with her at one time since I had left home for college in 2002. I drove her to school, picked her up, hung out with her third grade class, went shopping together, and went out to eat. And Thursday, June 5th, all of us sat around the table for a solid couple of hours just talking and sharing stories with each other. Looking back, being laid off and getting to spend that last week with Mom was a blessing from God. I will always be grateful for that.

I was also grateful for my boyfriend (now husband) who pulled me aside later and told me that from all appearances, Mom's heart attack was so massive that she probably did not suffer at all. I was grateful for the constant stream of family, friends, coworkers, and her former students that paid their respects at the funeral home. Although I have to say that seeing a group of her third grade students crying in the corner was both touching and gut-wrenching for me to see. One by one people came up to us with stories and memories of Mom. Many people made it a point to tell me how proud Mom always was of me. That meant more than I can say, given how bad I was feeling about my last words to her. I hoped she knew how much I loved her and how proud I was to be her daughter.

The time since Mom's death has been a time of reflection and memories for me. It is not unusual for me to smile at a memory of us baking cookies, having a pillow fight, finding the best sheet to use for fort building, and having a picnic in the park by the playground. She would help me plan and throw massive Christmas parties in high school for fifty people and not blink an eye. She had this amazing ability to always have the appetizers coming out of the oven just when supplies were running low. I don't think anyone ever left one of her events not feeling well fed and appreciated. I vividly remember shopping trips to Pittsburgh and my disdain for listening on the radio to Delilah After Dark on the hour's ride home. Now, if I could have one more shopping trip with her, I would gladly listen to Delilah. I would even crank that easy listening music up so the whole world could hear. Most importantly, I remember how Mom was always there for me when I needed support. She was there for the school romance breakups, for the life lessons I may have chosen to learn the hard way, and in the crowd for every play I was in and every ball game I played. I even joke that the little voice inside that tells me right from wrong got just a little bit louder after her passing. Anytime I was about to do something that may be a bit questionable I can almost hear her call me a "twit" (a common favorite expression of hers for both me and her students when acting ornery!)

It is also just as likely that in a private moment I will break down in tears if I hear certain songs on the radio or my iPod. Petula Clark's Downtown was a big favorite of Mom's and has the ability to reduce me to a puddle pretty much instantly. I still have nightmares where Mom is with me and I know she is about to suffer her fatal heart attack, but she refuses to go with me to the hospital. Or the dream where I know she needs me and I am in a maze of some sort and cannot find my way to her. There are times when I close my eyes to go to sleep and the image of her lying there dead on the floor jumps into my brain. I have yet to find anything to easily remove it when that happens. I missed her terribly when I planned my wedding this past summer. I think she would have approved of my effort, and hopefully she liked the flowers. Mom had a green thumb and a true love for flowers. I am lucky if I know the difference between a rose and a tulip.

Mom's passing helped shape my life and thinking in a number of ways. First, I took a step back and evaluated my career path. Prior to her death, I had been in a career that everyone said I would be great at, but that I truly hated. I realized that life is too short to not do something you are passionate about, so now I am in nursing school and hoping to be in a position to do something meaningful with my work day, every day. Second, I am more aware of what I say to people. I never go to sleep without telling my husband that I love him. I never hang up the phone with Dad without those words either. I no longer take it for granted that there will be a later to tell those closest to me that they are loved and appreciated. Third, Mom has given me a whole new perspective on death. It was once something that I feared, like most people do. Now, I think about how Mom is in Heaven, in no pain and surrounded by perfection and love. The rest of us are still here living life, and going through day to day in a world that can be full of love, but also violence, pain and suffering. There is a song that says, "God only cries for the living, because it is the living that are so far away." I believe that to be true. I find great comfort in the idea that Mom is in Heaven with her parents, family, and friends that have gone before, and she is patiently waiting for her husband and the little "twit" to join her in due time. Until then, I know I have her love in my heart to guide me. Unless I let her memory die, she will never be truly gone.

Laura Smith Lance

So Many Losses
Denise Keyser

It was February 9, 1987. I was in my Biology class. I had a horrible feeling and looked at the clock. It was a little after 10 a.m. After school was dismissed, I got on the bus. Just as the bus was about to pull away, I thought to myself, "Oh, shit! I'm supposed to go visit my mom at the hospital." I was too embarrassed to ask the bus driver to stop the bus so I could get off. I figured that I would just go tomorrow. It had been two weeks since I went to see her so what was another day? Her health had been steadily deteriorating, so at that moment I felt so guilty. A friend of mine sitting next to me asked me how my mom was doing. My mouth just took over and the words, "She's doing much better now" came out. I thought to myself, "What was I saying? I have no idea how she is doing."

My usual one and a half block walk home from the bus stop was unusually lonely. I was about a half block away when I saw someone familiar walking down from my driveway. No one was ever home when I got home from school. I could already tell from the tall slender figure that it was my oldest brother. Billy is nine years older than I am, and I looked up to him. He was married just six months ago. So seeing him walking toward me was a surprise, but not in a good way. I had an eerie feeling, but I couldn't quite place it. Billy approached me somberly. I cannot remember what he said. I just know that it was about my mom being dead. I realized walking into my house that it was filled with people, all crying, all looking at me. Here I was at fifteen years of age being told that my mother was dead. I am the youngest of three...two boys and a girl.

My mom was forty-eight years old. She died of non-Hodgkins lymphoma. She fell in the shower in June of 1986 and was dead eight months later. My life would be forever changed with one sentence: Mommy died. My brother, whom I looked up to, probably idolized, altered my life, and he didn't even know it. Many years later I found out that my poor brother had the awful misfortune of being the first one to see her like that in her hospital bed. He found her and then wanted to be the one to tell me. He had to tell me the news because I forgot and got on the bus. Now, I know that it was a blessing in disguise. I didn't have to be told by a stranger from the hospital staff; rather my big brother told me and comforted me. I don't remember him ever hugging me until that day, and I will never forget it. She was buried on Valentine's Day 1987.

Immediately after she died, everything fell apart. It all started previously when my grandfather decided to sell his house to my mother if he could remain living with us. When she passed away, my grandfather tried to get my dad and me evicted from the house. I remember going with my dad to the lawyer's office and at sixteen trying to explain to him what the lawyer was telling him. My father had me sign my mother's name on a will to make sure that the house would be left to the children. Then, he would have us sign the house over to him. This worked. We were able to stay in the house and that infuriated my grandfather. He would never speak to us again and moved out one day without notice.

After my mother died, my father suddenly fell apart and decided that I would be the "woman of the house"...almost a substitute for my mother. I remember my dad saying, "Thank God I have Denise." He spent most of his nights at home getting drunk. Twice he threatened to kill himself until I told him that I needed him. It felt like he thought of me more of a wife than a daughter. I was to cook for him, clean for him, go out to dinner and the movies with him.

It wasn't the first time in my young life that I didn't express my feelings. My mother had been hitting me for as long as I remember. My dad yelled at her one time about it. I was nine and was so scared to have a tooth pulled at the dentist. My mother wouldn't go into the treatment room and hold my hand. Instead for embarrassing her, she beat on me on the way home, while driving. I still have the scar on my face. There was a time that I had to go to school late because she hit me so hard that my nose kept bleeding. I had a hard time understanding why after her death, whenever her name was mentioned, she was spoken of as if she should be canonized.

My dad worked two shifts and didn't come home until very late. My mother's brother, eighteen years her junior, lived with us. I look back at him now as a "father substitute" for me. I probably looked for his qualities when I married.

A few months prior to my mom's death, my oldest brother got married and moved out. After my mom died, my second oldest brother decided to move out also. So I ended up living with an angry grandfather and a sad father. Our home went from "lots of activity" to absolutely none. I became distant and withdrawn. I wanted to be independent and didn't want the responsibilities heaped onto me as a mother-substitute. My dad's rule was: "If you're not out of the house by 4 p.m., then you're not out at all." My brothers seemed to have no idea of what my life was like or what was happening to me.

I was not permitted to go to college but had to find employment. When I was twenty years old, I secretly signed up for the community college and at age twenty-one, I enrolled there.

My mother's death was the beginning of my inner feelings of abandonment and having NO support from anyone. After I married and had my second baby in 2007, I developed "postpartum depression" and my husband hired a wonderful woman to help me with the house and the children. It was through her caring and guidance that I decided that I needed to get some help from a counselor. I knew that it was time for me to go "back" in my past and with help, to resolve the issues that had been repressed for so long.

Denise Keyser

SAYING GOODBYE TO OUR PARENTS
Nanette Schaller & Maria Greco Cox

One of life's greatest blessings is the gift of friendship. One of my most special friendships is that of the relationship I have shared with Nanette Greco Schaller. Our relationship began when I was the guidance counselor for her two beloved sons, Jerry and Vincent. They were the type of students who really didn't need me as a counselor...they were extremely intelligent, diligent students, well-mannered and gracious. In other words, they were a beautiful reflection of their parents and the love and values with which they were raised.

After her sons graduated and were on their way to medical school, my friendship with Nanette blossomed into a lasting relationship that has grown with respect and caring for each other. As women do, we shared our life's ups and downs and soon discovered that we shared one very special similarity in the memories of our Italian heritage and our beautiful parents.

We were talking about the fact that we are now "orphans"...adult children who have lost both parents. I asked Nanette to tell me about her mother and father, and she gave me two eulogies that were read at their respective funerals. I decided to share these with the readers of Moments Like This as they really give us a view into the lives of the Greco family in Philadelphia. The first one was written by Nanette's sister, Maria, and really helps us to know their beloved mother, Lucille Greco.

Sylvia Silvetti Havlish

EULOGY FOR LUCILLE GRECO

My mother was the most kind, gentle and loving woman. She touched each of us in a unique and special way. We have been changed and enhanced by her kindness, her gentleness, and her love for us. My mother was a creative and talented person who shared generously of her talents. I doubt if there is anyone here who did not benefit from her generosity. Perhaps it was a beautiful item of clothing which she sewed for you or someone in your family; it may have been a plate of her cookies; one of her paintings;or the sound of her beautiful voice in song.

Perhaps she was there for you with her listening ear, her prayers or her patient understanding of our humanness. She gave lovingly for the sheer joy of giving. As the Bible instructs us, she was truly a cheerful giver who took great pleasure in giving.

My mother was a study in simplicity. She really enjoyed the simple things in life, whether it was a beautiful sunset, the roses Pop picked for her, a walk in the woods or by the ocean, and always the presence of family and friends. My mother possessed great wisdom. She understood clearly and responded passionately to the complexity of the human spirit. With patience, she sought always to understand, to give counsel, and when necessary, to forgive.

Although she raised four fiery daughters, my mother was a peaceful woman who truly found goodness in everyone. Temperamentally, my brother, Emile, was most like her. She had an intense and abiding faith, and it was not unusual for all of us to ask her to pray when we needed God's help. Somehow it felt as if she might have a little more influence with Him!

Mother was passionate about life and thankful for every day. She went through life with an incredible amount of energy and fully expected that energy to return even to the end of her life. Despite her great faith, my mother did not "go gently into that good night." There was so much more she wanted to do, to see, to share more moments with all of us. Her stamina in the face of overwhelming physical odds was a testimony to the value she placed on life.

And so I believe this to be her legacy to all of us who loved her. Celebrate each day. Take joy in simple things, love deeply, passionately, unequivocally and see the goodness in all you meet. Believe in yourself, trust in God, in whom she knew all things were possible. Can it be so that eighty-one years is such a brief moment in time? I think not. My mother, Lucille Greco, will live on in our hearts and in the memories that we will continue to share with our children and their children. And so, my dear, sweet Mommy, now is the hour when we must say goodbye and say as you have said so often to all of us: May God bless, guide and protect you. Know that we will truly miss you and that we will never ever forget you. Your loves lives on in all of us.

Nanette also shared with me the eulogy for her father, Vincent Greco. I do not know to whom to give credit for these words, but they capture the essence of this dear man.

EULOGY FOR VINCENT GRECO

As I was trying to find the words to express the essence of my father and the landscape of his long lifetime in a few brief moments, the passage on love from Corinthians came into my mind. It occurred to me that in the eighty-eight years that Pop lived, he saw many changes…giant leaps in transportation and telecommunications, two world wars, several smaller wars, the great depression, various popes and presidents…to name a few. I believe that in the ever-changing world in which he lived, my father was a consistent presence in that world. Throughout he remained a fine, Christian gentleman. The words from Corinthians will help me explain those words:

"Love is patient; love is kind; it is not self-seeking; it is not easily angered;

it keeps no record of wrongs; it always protects; always trusts, always hopes and always perseveres."

Throughout his life, Pop was a thoughtful and loving man. My mother did not have to wait for a special occasion for him to express his love. Time after time, in the midst of the business of everyday life, Pop would appear carrying a single coral rose. In the summer he would cut one from the garden before he entered the house; in the winter he stopped at the florist on the way home from Mass. I am sure we can all remember a time when Pop would present something that we fancied: warm soft pretzels, "kitkats," donuts, or whatever we enjoyed. Pop took pleasure in pleasing.

Pop was always a kind, gentle man, soft spoken and slow to anger. I can honestly say that in the fifty-four years I had the privilege of knowing him, I never heard his voice raised in anger. Daddy was not about anger; he was about love and support and family and caring and yes, romance!

Daddy lived long enough to learn from his children. Because he was such a decent man, he found it difficult at first to accept that some of his children would travel down unusual and unexpected paths. Love never left the equation, however. Understanding, compassion, and acceptance took time, but they eventually came. Daddy became a most non-judgmental man, no "black and white" thinking for him. He acquired a wonderful ability to see and appreciate life's gray areas. In that acquisition he became his most loving and Christian self.

His patience showed itself most clearly in his later years, first, in his ongoing devotion to my Mother as she became more and more frail. She always lived at home, and he always cared for her lovingly, kindly and patiently. In the last year and a half of his own life, he had to be so patient with all the physical changes that he encountered. Getting dressed and getting around became more and more difficult for him, but I never heard him complain. His only concern was that he may have become a burden to us.

However, in addition to being a very loving man, he was also a very loved man. In the last days of his life, since November of 1997, he lived with my sister Nanette and her husband Jerry. In their home he knew deep commitment to his well-being and a daily dose of kindness. In the morning when my father awakened, Jerry would show up at his bedroom door with a cup of coffee. Later, as he failed even more, Jerry would bring breakfast to his room as he waited to be dressed to come downstairs. Nanette could not do enough for him. Day after day she found hundreds of ways to make his life comfortable and secure and yes, even fun! For as long as he was able, Nanette would catch him up in the whirlwind of her life, whether it was going to a job site or wherever her business took her. Daddy spent his last days surrounded by life and he loved it.

Pop never lost his sense of humor, and cherished every day, every smile, every amusing moment that came his way. He was never a "dying man." He was alive and fully living in the present. To the very end he dressed in a starched shirt and the inevitable tie. What a lovely consistent memory we have of that. Even when he was sitting on the patio with no real agenda for the day, he was dressed up. It will always make me smile as I remember Pop in that way, dressed for the occasion, the daily greeting of a new day.

A little over a week ago, Nanette told me I should come if I wanted to say goodbye, since his days were growing short. I had always been afraid in the face of death, but I will forever be grateful for this last week I spent with my father. Death no longer frightens me. I watched as in this last week in a warm room in the middle of things, with music playing and a fire going, and life continuing around him, he very slowly and quietly in his own way moved away from us and away from his tired old body to the beauty of his every-youthful spirit. In his last moments, he kissed each of us and inevitably made us laugh. It was a peaceful death when it came. As he and the household slept, as he had prayed that it would happen, he quietly left us.

In the end that was Pop's heartfelt wish: that his children and his friends would learn from his consistent example, the example of a fine, Christian gentleman. Pop was a simple man, self-contained but with such an incredible presence. I always felt that when he entered a room, the air around him changed and we all sensed the change.

Can it be that eighty-eight years is such a brief moment in time? I think not. My father, Vincent Greco, will live on in our hearts and in the memories that we have and will continue to share with our children and grandchildren. And so my Sweet Poppy, now is the hour when we must say goodbye. May God bless, guide and protect you. Know that we will never forget you. Your love lives on in each of us.

I want to thank Nanette and her sisters for sharing these beautiful memories with me and with all of us. As we have told each other countless times, we were such lucky, lucky daughters. God blessed both of us with incredible, loving parents. May they all rest in peace...and find each other and compare notes about their daughters!

Sylvia Silvetti Havlish
February 2012

My Dad, John Howard
(1920-1978)
Ruth Howard Marcon

John Howard was the son of Syrian immigrants. He was born in Allentown, Pennsylvania, and left it only to serve in the U. S. Navy during World War II. He served on the USS Iowa.

After the war he returned to Allentown to be with my mom and me. In the early years of marriage, Dad drove my mother to exasperation because he liked to gamble. But he always won at craps. And as mom would say later, "He was a good provider." He worked hard and saved money. He paid cash for our house; he paid cash for family cars; he paid cash for our college tuition. No business or bank was going to get a penny more than it deserved.

Dad had his own business as a car mechanic. He could fix anything. He later worked at Bethlehem Steel. He left the Steel and started his own used car business. Our family cars were Chevys and Fords. He would die all over again if he knew that we're driving BMWs and Volvos.

Dad liked Westerns...especially the Duke, John Wayne. He liked dark chocolate Cella cherries, even though our best candy shop in town had better ones. After he retired he made fruit and vegetable shopping a weekly labor of love. My mother often scolded him for buying too much of a good thing...or for buying fruit out of season. I didn't mind. I loved cherries and strawberries, and he always made sure I got my fill. One of my strongest memories is of his coming to my house after shopping at the Farmer's Market. My image of him is strong and clear. He is standing in the kitchen doorway holding up a large, green bell pepper and saying, "Isn't this beautiful!"

Dad died of lung cancer. He told us of his cancer after a traditional

Labor Day picnic supper. He died December first. My mother cared for him at home with help from my brother, David, who was living at home at the time. We all watched his decline with fear and sadness. Dad couldn't leave his bed at Thanksgiving. I can still remember the sadness and burden of that day. A happy family celebration couldn't be.

In those last weeks I actually resented the friends and family who came to see him. I felt that they robbed us of time with him…time that we needed more. I learned what the words "anticipatory grief" meant. We all were tired and tense from watching and waiting for his last breath. I wanted him to die so he wouldn't have to suffer any longer, yet I didn't want to lose him. What happened to be the last night of his life, my mother was exhausted and needed to sleep. Before she did, she told me that if anything happened I should wake her. I sat in the chair in their bedroom. Mom slept on the couch in the living room, not far from their first-floor bedroom. I sat in the upholstered chair in their bedroom, watching and waiting, and afraid something would happen and I wouldn't know.

I don't remember waking Mom. But I must have because we were in the room together when Dad died. His breathing got quieter and breaths were farther apart until there were no more breaths. It was a peaceful passing. My fear ceased. We had said our goodbyes and had important talks over the last few weeks of his illness. Now we kissed him for the last time.

Dad had always said he didn't want us to grieve after he died. But we couldn't help it. He loved us imperfectly, but we knew he loved us. I felt the loss more than I ever imagined I would. I was sad and depressed for months and months. I went through the motions of Christmas that year only because I had three young kids. I don't remember when the sadness ebbed enough that I felt "normal." I stopped grieving, and I stopped mourning a long time ago. It's now thirty-three years since Dad died. But as I write this piece, it feels not that long ago. I'm crying, and I miss him.

Ruth Howard Marcon   February 2012

WAYNE SCHLEGEL
Doug Schlegel & Cyndi O'Hara

I've always felt it was so moving when a family member is actually able to not only write a eulogy for a beloved parent, but also finds the courage and strength to actually read it at the funeral service. The following two eulogies were written and presented by the adult children of Wayne Schlegel. I had the pleasure of working with his wife, Gloria, when I was a teacher and counselor in a local high school. Although I never had the experience of knowing Wayne during his lifetime, after reading the two eulogies, I have learned so much about this wonderful man and his grateful family. Wayne's son, Doug, wrote the first one...and his daughter, Cyndi O'Hara, shares her memories in the second writing.

Sylvia Silvetti Havlish

DAD...DOUG SCHLEGEL

This is one of those moments in life that I expect to remember clearly...standing in front of a fine group of people and being able to talk about one of the best guys most of us will come across in life. The number of you here is a testimony to him and a gift to his family and really to all of us. As I was thankfully able to tell him in the days before he passed, he leaves a wide and deep legacy.

Ok, so let's set some expectations up front. As I share a few things for the next ten minutes or so, it's pretty likely I'm not going to make it without choking up, so apologies in advance. And I am not quite ready to use past tense all the time when talking about Dad. It's not avoiding reality or being silly, it's just that he's going to be in my mind a lot for the rest of my days, so present tense also works just fine for me. But I am aiming my thought to be on the lighter side, so hopefully that comes through.

For those of you who have spoken in a moment like this about a loved one, you may have found it a challenge to whittle down to a reasonable length, the things you want to add to people's memories about them…without putting everyone to sleep or taking hours to do it. Dad is known well by most of you so I know that you have your own memories…and maybe I can add just one or two more.

So what do you say about a guy like Wayne? Well, this is my attempt.

He Is A Fighter.

He locked his knees for hours on end at the top of many a telephone pole in all kinds of weather until the work was done.

Just look at what he survived. In fact, our son, Cody carries around as inspiration the list that Mom wisely kept of all his medical issues. A sampling of what he overcame: 5 heart surgeries; over 10 other surgeries; 4 significant infections; several bouts with cancer; a few strokes, and so on.

And let's not forget about Mom's huge role in getting him through those times.

He Inspires.

With all those things he fought off, how often did he complain? Has anyone ever really heard him do so? He was more concerned about how his illness was affecting you than how it was affecting him.

He dealt with and, most importantly, stayed positive during these many health battles. To me, that is an inspiration, and I hope I can be half as good a patient as he was. Julie tells me that I am a wimp even when I get a simple cold, so there is probably no hope there!

Even in the most recent days, he was prone to ask about how someone else was doing or "crack a joke." A good example of this was that only two weeks ago, our son, Cody, was working on his Jeep trying to take the doors off. While doing so he dropped a door on his foot...big ouch! Dad's line to him over the telephone was: "You know what I do when a door is falling? I get out of the way!" Good advice.

Some of my last images of him are, despite all that was going on, how he would raise his head and smile.

HE SERVED OTHERS.

The armed forces, the Masonic Temple, Lions Club, St. John's United Church of Christ, Little League, the town zoning board, his friends, family, coworkers and on and on.

I remember him shoveling/snow-blowing the entire block storm after storm, winter after winter until his legs no longer allowed it. He led by example.

For how many of you has he done something to help out? (Many people raised their hands.) Nicer still is how many of you have done the same for him and others..."passing it on" like that is wonderfully typical of our hometown, Emmaus.

HE COULD FIX JUST ABOUT ANYTHING.

Mom and Dad built their own home "for crying out loud"...and it is still as solid as if it was built yesterday.

A recent example is Rory's new house in Philadelphia when a few of us went to see it for the first time last Christmas. It was at that moment that the electricity went out on one floor. So, "who ya gonna call??" Call 1-800-Wayne Can Fix It! By phone, he walked us through a circuit breaker/wiring repair sight unseen. Of course he said he would have done it without turning the electricity off, but Bob, Rory, and I weren't quite ready to be "human light bulbs" that day.

He knew a lot and shared it with anyone who asked. I have saved thousands of dollars using what I learned from him...which is good, since I am "cheap!"

He Said "I Love You" A Lot.

Not all fathers have the ability to say "I love you" or the inclination to say it. Thankfully, not him!

Mom, Cyndi and I, as well as the grandchildren, all heard it and knew it and felt it.

We say it around our house a lot. What a wonderful gift for Mom and Dad to give to their family.

While speaking of things he would say, when I think of Dad, what phrases come to mind as something Wayne would always say? A few of my favorites are:

"Wos comma do?" Pennsylvania Dutch for "what can you do?" He thought of that phrase as "...you can't control everything, so enjoy what you have and get on with it."

"You gotta have the right tools...with the right tool, you can fix anything!" This seems like a good analogy on life.

"If you're gonna buy something, wait till you have the money and get the best." This is also great advice.

And, the most famous of his lines, "No problem!"

Can you fix the sink? NP
Can you re-wire the whole house? NP
Can I have a couple of bucks?   NP
Dad, sorry about the new dent in your truck. NP
…although that took a few days!

I know that God has some things lined up for him to do, and when God asks him to do them, I am sure Dad is going to respond…all together now…NO PROBLEM!

These are some of the things which will make me think of him often. While my weekly chats with him won't be over the phone anymore, I am thinking they'll happen ever more often as has been the case for the last few days.

A last brief story to close before Cyndi shares some of her thoughts:

A few of you may remember an article in the local paper several years ago, which spoke of the four Schlegel brothers who went into the armed service to serve in World War II before they received their diplomas. They were Ray, Buddy, Lee, Dad as well as Auntie's husband, Uncle Norman. The article told of their pride in receiving the diplomas fifty years later and recounted their war-time experiences and feelings from many years ago.

What struck me was that at the very end of the article, Dad was quoted as having "lived the American dream" saying,

"We were told to come home, get a job, get a house, build a family and live happily ever after…and that's just about what we did!"

Yup…that's exactly what he did.

And by Mom and Dad doing it so well, they made the same thing possible for us.

That's a legacy to be proud of. I love you, Dad.

Eulogy for her Dad
Cyndi O'Hara

I didn't realize it was going to be this difficult…to put in writing how I feel about my Dad and to keep it shorter than two hours!

When I think about Dad, there are streams of thoughts, memories, and special moments. What he has taught me and what he has meant to us as a family are some of the things I want to share with you at this time. Thank you for indulging me.

Dad. He was larger than life…one of the truly "good guys." I have always admired his strength: his physical strength…climbing trees, building our home, and climbing ladders to work on the roof. Of course, Dad's descent from the ladder was not like the normal person. He rapelled down the ladder using only his hands, while his feet hung on either side of the ladder. Bob called him Tarzan.

He began his job as a lineman for the telephone company and retired as a manager. He was climbing telephone poles long before bucket trucks existed. I asked him just two weeks ago, "Did you really like climbing up so high on those poles?" He answered, "It was my job and secondly, I was good at it." Dad never boasted about the things he did. The lesson he imparted was not through lecturing or repetition of the usual advice…it was one of setting an example.

Wayne's word was better than a signed contract. He was unselfish with his time for his family and others. I remember many phone calls he received asking for his help, i.e., trouble with my phone, electrical problems, requests for cutting down huge trees, help with moving, helping to maintain a huge garden for an old friend, and so many others. He always said "YES" and never expected anything in return. His answer was "No Problem!" We gave him a tee shirt with just those words on it, because that was our Dad. He could do anything and fix anything. As I got older, I worked with him on some repair jobs at our home. He said "…if 'plan A' doesn't work, sometimes you have to go to 'plan B' or 'C'." I was with him at "Plan A" but didn't get the "Plan B" or "C" gene! He set an example of doing a job right no matter how long it took, and in his own words, "Never do something half-assed!"

His strength was not only physical. He had a strong spiritual strength. Again, he never really talked about it, he lived it. How else could he have gotten through all his physical and life-threatening medical problems and crises if he didn't have a strong faith? He lived it by being active in his church, by becoming "Worshipful Master" of the Masons and by living his faith quietly and privately. Several years ago on one of his many emergency room admissions, it was in the middle of the night. Mom and I had to leave while they were doing the paperwork to admit him to the hospital. I asked him the next day after learning that he had spent four hours in the ER alone, "Dad, you were alone a long time. What did you do?" He answered simply, "I prayed."

His strength was also in his humor and his incredible good nature. I've never heard him gossip or say an unkind word about someone. He never once complained about all the pain and problems he endured. When someone asked how he was, he would answer, "I'm in good shape for the shape I'm in!" He never asked, "Why me?" He always looked like "a million bucks"....totally belying how difficult it was for him to just get up and move. He had a smile for everyone... and he loved women, especially the pretty ones! He was nice to all the medical personnel and nurses, but if they were attractive, he flirted and smiled even more for them!

He loved to dance and was always dragging Mom on the dance floor. If she tired, he would grab one of their friends and continue on. He had a beautiful voice and sang in the Lions Chorus...although I didn't get that gene either! He sometimes said things he pulled out of nowhere and surprised us all. We would laugh in disbelief and in appreciation of his humor. He loved to travel and to party. Mom and Dad hosted many parties. He made several of their costumes for Halloween parties. His most famous outfit was the "dice" they hid in…and squirted water through the holes if anyone got too close.

For his 60th birthday, he went on a hot air balloon ride and had a belly dancer with him. He loved that!

But by far, his greatest love was for his family. He loved his grandchildren. He was so proud of their accomplishments and the kind of people they have grown to be. He loved hearing stories about Cody…especially playing soccer which brought back memories of watching Doug play soccer. Cody, you were always caring and helpful with grandpa…being his "crutch" to lean on when they visited you in the Netherlands without even being asked! Tia, his only granddaughter…he was so very proud of you and loved holding his baby girl when you were little. You are so special to him…and those extra hugs and "love you Papa" melted his heart.

Rory and Rhett…Dad was so thrilled when he knew he was going to have a grandchild. But when you were both born, he couldn't get enough of you! He would come over several times a week to hold you, walk you, and just look at you. As you grew, he loved having you for sleepovers, taking you to fun places and letting you stay up late, playing cards. Grandma and Grandpa's house was a special place. He went to almost every baseball, basketball, soccer, and lacrosse game you had. He sometimes traveled quite a distance for tournaments and "away" games. You could always find him at a baseball or soccer game by following the trail of peanut shells!

He was so very proud of you both and always loved your visits and calls. His constant question when I talked to him was, "What have you heard from the boys?" He loved hearing about your latest adventures and travels. He was always in your corner and your constant fan. And Katie, he loved you from the beginning and told me, "Tell Rory she's a keeper. Don't let her get away!" He couldn't make it to your wedding, but we carried him there in our hearts.

And Doug, peachy creamy! He was so incredibly proud of the man and father you have become. When you were born, he was like the "second coming!" He had a son he could play with and do all the "manly" kind of things like snow mobiles, motor bikes, baseball, skeet shooting, fishing, and passing on his talent of working with his hands. He said many times how much he cherished and loved helping you repair things in your house and building things together. A few years ago you did some work in my house and Dad could only supervise, but you could see the pride in his face when he looked at me and said, "Doug knows what he is doing, and he does it well!"

His very favorite times were when all of his family was together in one place. He just sat back and listened to the banter and laughter, and during those times, we knew he felt that he had everything he could ever want...right in front of him. He loved Bob and Julie... respected their accomplishments, proud of their roles as parents, and blessed to see that they made his children feel supported and loved.

And Mom! He loved and was totally still in love with Mom... from their wedding day, through sixty-five years together. You could see it in the way he looked at her. The love shone through in his eyes. There is no doubt in my mind that if it were not for his love for my mother and his will to be with her that we would not have had him with us as long as we did. For the first fifty-five years of his life, he was very healthy and took care of her. After that, there were more medical issues...some life-threatening and debilitating. Mom took care of him, nursed him, became his "record keeper" and his advocate. He became dependent on her but tried very hard not to burden her. Mom, you are a strong woman...whether you realize that or not, and I think he was, in some ways, preparing you for when he could not be here. His greatest gift to us was his deep, caring, protection, commitment and love for Mom. Their marriage and the love they shared is an incredible inspiration. What greater gift could he give us?

As for me, he was my first "best guy." He was never critical of me, even when I went through my "hippie time" in Boston. He never asked me to change or be someone else. He taught me about boxing and football, house stuff and gardening. I helped him plant and harvest what he grew, and when I started my own garden, I had some questions. The best one was, "Dad, my garden has tons of weeds. Why don't you have any?" He looked at me with his patient smile and said, "I pull em!"

As a daughter, what have I learned from my father? So many things...to name a few...he showed me how it feels to be loved unconditionally. He was the standard against which I would judge all men. He taught me what kind of man to choose to be the father of my children. He let me know that while I may not be the center of someone else's world, I was the center of his. He was the safe spot I could always turn to. There is no measure as to how very much I will miss him answering the phone with an excited, loving, "Hi, honey!" every time I called...even though I just spoke to him the day before. Mom has said many times, "You were his princess; you could do no wrong." Everyone should have someone in their life that feels that way about them. I had my Dad.

His greatest gift to us was the gift of himself...simply an extraordinary role model. And knowing, without a doubt, that we were loved and cherished by this wonderful man was the greatest blessing we could receive.

Thank you, Dad. I will miss you terribly, but you will always be in my heart.

He fought the good fight, he finished the race and he kept the faith. He is free of pain now and at peace.

I love you, Dad.

Gloria Schlegel
Postscript for a Beautiful Lady
June 5, 1026 – February 28, 2012
Sylvia Silvetti Havlish

In my last bereavement group session in November, 2011, Gloria Schlegel rushed over to hand me an envelope containing the eulogies written by her children for her late husband, Wayne. You have just read them in the preceding story. She was so excited to share with me and with my "future readers" the heartfelt feelings for her husband. I thanked her for contributing to the book I was working on, and she hugged me and held me tightly. She shared with me that she felt so much better since joining the group and felt that she had made new bonds with the other lovely people in the room. She told me that she was about to make a flight to Texas for the Christmas holidays to the home of her son, Doug. The rest of the Pennsylvania family would join a week or so later for the actual week of Christmas. I told her that I was proud of her for her incredibly positive attitude, her willingness to help the other group members when she sensed that they needed a hug or hand to hold, and that she was ready to make this trip and try to make the best of the first Christmas holiday since her husband's death.

As I was straightening up the room before I locked up for the evening, I kept thinking about what an inspiration Gloria had been in this group. It isn't often that a "newly bereaved" widow can give of herself to help others who are grieving. But she did…and often. She had a peacefulness about her by the end of the group that is unusual after such a short time. I made a promise to myself that I would make sure that I contacted her after a few months to see how she was doing. I never got to talk with her again.

Gloria became ill the day after returning from her trip to Texas, and her downward spiral was amazingly fast. I had no idea what was happening in her life until her friend called to tell me that Gloria had passed away on February 28. I was in a state of shock.

But after the telephone call, Gloria's very last words to me came rushing back to my mind. "Sylvia," she said, "I've had such a good life. We had a wonderful, long marriage and a beautiful family. I am not afraid of dying, and now I know that Wayne will be there waiting for me." My response to her was something about hoping that she wasn't in any hurry to get there...but she just smiled, tilted her head and said, "When God is ready for me to join Wayne, I'll be ready."

According to Gloria's family, she was indeed peaceful and ready to be welcomed home. At her funeral service in her church, St. John's United Church of Christ in Emmaus, Pennsylvania, we were asked to read together the "Affirmation of Faith." I find it most fitting to close my story about Gloria with this powerful affirmation as it was written in her funeral service:

Pastor: Let us say again what we believe.

All: We believe there is no condemnation for those who are in Christ Jesus, and we know that in everything God works for good with those who love God, who are called according to God's purpose. We are sure that neither death, nor life, nor angels nor principalities, nor things present, nor things come, nor powers, nor height, nor depth, nor anything else in all creation, will be able to separate us from the love of God in Christ Jesus our Lord. Amen.
AMEN!

Sylvia Silvetti Havlish   March 4, 2012

My Last Year with Daddy
Jeanne Harakal

It was September of 1979, and I decided it was time for me to return home after living and working in Madrid, Spain for four years. My parents were thrilled that I was returning and would be living with them while I searched for a new job and a new apartment. Little did I know then that it would be my father's last year of life. I look back now and truly believe that a greater force brought me home that fall.

It was a tough time looking for a job teaching English as a second language. No matter where I applied, I was rejected. My dad supported me through all of my frustration and told me not to worry. He knew something would come along for me.

In the meantime, he took a day off from work, and we went shopping at Hess's Department Store in downtown Allentown. I wanted a pair of "Jordache" jeans but couldn't afford the $26 price tag. It was a lot of money for someone with no job. But, he bought them for me, and I have them to this day. They were one of the last things he gave to me. After more shopping we ended the morning with a lunch at the famous Patio Restaurant in Hess's. We had lunch, a drink, and some strawberry pie. It is one of my favorite memories with him.

About a month after getting home, our dog, Duffy, was having trouble chewing. He was my dad's best buddy...the only other "boy" in the house. He loved him so much. We found that Duffy's jaw was broken in three places, and he was now half his regular weight. We were told he could not withstand the surgery and that he should be euthanized. My father weighed the decision and discussed it with the family. We all decided it was the best direction to take. Later, my dad regretted the decision and felt that he might have been able to nurse Duffy back to health. We wanted to get him a new puppy, but he said that no other dog could replace Duffy. It was so upsetting to see my dad so sad that his little buddy was no longer with us. I felt helpless.

I finally landed a job at a jewelry store as a sales clerk. Shortly afterwards, I was offered a full-time position as a management trainee. I was happy to have employment, and Dad was happy for me as well. He came into the store and picked out a few things for my mom. She always liked jewelry.

Christmas was right around the corner. I had a new job and was earning good money. I was home for the holidays and enjoying a new life in the states. Life was good…

But then came the news right before Christmas that some sort of growth was felt in my father's abdomen, and he was scheduled for exploratory surgery after the holidays. How could this be? Cancer? He was only fifty-six years old. So many thoughts ran through my head. I was only twenty-six years old, and my father was supposed to be around for a lot longer. He was supposed to be a part of my children's lives. I wanted him to play softball with them as he had with me. I wanted him to teach them how to tie seaman's knots as he had for me. I wanted him to go along on hikes and scout trips and whatever else he did with me. I wanted all of us to do that together. When I look back now, I feel as if my children have been robbed of knowing what a great father and grandfather they missed.

Christmas Eve came, and I had to work until six o'clock. When I got home, I asked my dad if he would go to church with me for the last service at eight o'clock. My mother always spent the entire evening at church every Christmas Eve since she sang in the choir, but my dad never went to church. He felt that he had done so many bad things during the war that God would not forgive him, and he had no right to be in church. This night, however, he agreed to go with me. When we arrived, the only seats left were in the very first pew in the front of the church. My father always joked that the church was going to collapse if he went to church. The minister smiled at both of us sitting in the front pew. Once again, I did not realize that it would be the last time I would be in church with him and his last Christmas.

We were so hopeful when the time came for his surgery. They removed a tumor in his colon and found that the cancer had already metastasized quite a bit, including to his liver. There was nothing more to do surgically, and they informed us that he had eight to twelve months to live. They recommended that he take chemotherapy to give him more time.

I visited my dad in the hospital while he was recuperating from surgery and all he did was think about others. He asked about my job and kept track of when I was getting paid. He always focused on others, not on his own problems.

He decided to give chemotherapy a try, but it was tough on him. He was sick all the time. We decided to get some marijuana for him to try to ease the nausea. He never smoked but was willing to try. He would go downstairs to his bar in the basement and smoke a joint to make him feel better. It never really did a lot to help him.

As the time went on, my dad continued to lose weight. He was in pain and could no longer eat and drink the things he wanted. His condition continued to deteriorate until he had to return for a colostomy surgery in May. My dad was beginning to realize that his time was limited. When he returned home, he decided that it was time to arrange his funeral. My mother drove him to the funeral home, and he picked out his casket. He joked that he spent more money than he had intended but had chosen the prettiest casket with a blue lining! He wanted to make sure that we would not have to do anything when the time came. Again, he was thinking of everyone else but himself. He wanted everyone he loved to be cared for when he was gone.

The next few months we watched my father wither away. He was a professional weight lifter and body builder and had always been so muscular. He was 165 pounds when he was lifting, and it was all muscle. Now his muscles were almost non-existent and atrophied, and he weighed at least sixty pounds less.

He told us he wanted to die at home and not in the hospital. My mother ordered a hospital bed, and we set it up in a bedroom at the house. My mother and my sister, Dawn, took a leave of absence from their workplaces so that they could care for him at home. They were helped by the visiting nurses and the hospice staff who assisted. I felt so guilty that I could not take time off from my new job. I couldn't afford to with having to pay for a newly rented apartment, and I knew I wouldn't have a job to go back to if I asked for a month off. I felt there was nothing I could do. The guilt still remains that I wasn't there to help.

The month of August arrived. This was our family month of birthdays and anniversaries. My birthday was August 1, my parent's anniversary was August 4, my mom's birthday was August 7 and my dad's was on August 12, and their only granddaughter's birthday was August 21. By this time my father was so thin and in terrible pain. Each visit seemed worse. I tried to watch the news with him during one visit as it was always something we enjoyed together. But that night he said that he didn't care to watch it anymore since he would no longer be here, and it didn't matter what was going on. On another visit he wanted to take all of his pills to end his pain. We had to hide them from him.

For the last week of his life he was bedridden, and the cancer was starting to affect his brain. One night after work, I went to see him, and he was afraid of me. He didn't recognize me. I was so upset. I just wanted him to know me and talk to me one more time.

The next night I received a call at work to come and see him when I was able. My mom was afraid it was getting towards the end of his life. I arrived about ten-thirty, and he was able to talk to me and knew who I was. I wanted to stay for the night, but my brother-in-law was staying and told me to go home, get some sleep, and return in the morning.

At three a.m. I received a phone call from my mother who let me know that my dad had passed away. I went to the house and waited with everyone for the undertaker. I felt that I should have stayed through that night, but my family told me that it was better that I just remember him the way I left him that night…each saying we loved each other and would see each other soon.

The next few days were difficult with the memorial service and then the funeral. We invited everyone back to my mother's home and that was when I went out to the back yard and broke down sobbing uncontrollably. To my surprise, my mom came out and tried to comfort me. She said that my father had been suffering terribly and that he was now at peace and in a better place. I look back on that now and realize that we are often thinking more of ourselves when holding on to our loved ones instead of allowing them to go in peace. We hold on to them sometimes too long. My father held on until August 23, 1980. It was almost one year from the time I had returned home. They say that people can choose when they let go or hold on until a certain day before they pass away. With my dad always thinking of others, he wanted to make sure that he remained through all of the August "celebrations" before he let go.

All of this happened thirty-two years ago, but it remains in my mind like it was yesterday. I miss my daddy still so much and wish I could have him back with me for even one more day. When I think of how I raised my children, I can thank him for showing me the way to good parenting skills. He was selfless, always caring, but stern while teaching us right from wrong, but always admitted his imperfections along the way. He will always be my daddy, and I will always be his little girl.

Two Obituaries...And The "Rest of the Story"

Nancy Meck

When my parents passed away almost one year apart, the local newspaper carried their obituaries. The facts that the "rest of the world" reads carry only a small part of the stories of their lives. Their obituaries read as follows:

RUSSELL D. STERNER

Russell D. Sterner, 80, of Breinigsville, passed away Thursday, December 9, 2010 in Lehigh Valley Hospice, Allentown. Born in Bethlehem, he was a son of the late Orange R. and Hannah J. (Oakes) Sterner. He owned and operated an Exxon service station in Breinigsville and a Texaco Service Station in Allentown. He was a member of Grace Luteran Church in Macungie and was a 32nd degree Mason with the Emmaus Lodge #792 F & AM. He was well known in the Breinigsville area and was always willing to help those in need. He served in the U.S. Army during World War II.

(Following this summary of his life was a list of the survivors and the announcement of the funeral time.)

ELEANOR I. STERNER

Eleanor I. Sterner, 80, of Sinking Springs, formerly of Allentown, died Wednesday, February 16, 2011, in the Hospice House of St.

Luke's, Bethlehem. Born in Allentown, she was the daughter of the late Frederick E. and Rosie A. (Shaner) Smith. She worked in the housekeeping Department at Luther Crest, Allentown, for 17 years before retiring. She was a member of Grace Lutheran Church, Macungie, Red Hat Society, Allentown, and a lifetime member of the Allentown Senior Citizens. She was a loving mother, grandmother, and great-grandmother to be.

(Following this summary of her life was a list of the survivors and the announcement of the funeral time.)

⁓

When I attended two bereavement groups with my husband after both of these losses, the counselor, Sylvia, asked us to tell the group about our deceased loved ones. As I was writing out my notes for the group, I realized how very much there was to share about my parents that could never be seen in the obituaries. Here are my heartfelt memories of these special people.

My father, Russell Sterner, was so proud of being a Mason and of serving his country in World War II. He was a gentle soul, always willing to help others. Whether it was fixing cars, building houses or cooking our meals when my mother worked nights, he was always a willing and gracious helper. As his life progressed, he had to deal with the alcoholism that would become an intruder in our lives. But even through all this, he always took care of his family.

When he became ill, we all took turns visiting him at Cedarbrook Nursing Home as his dementia robbed him of his memory of our family life together. I remember how many places he took me, and we became very close. I was able to take him many places including baseball games, train rides, and trips to the Queen City Airport. He got to experience these places "through my eyes" in his later years. My father showed me unconditional love, just as Jesus showed that type of love to His children. I miss my father.

⁓

My mother, Eleanor Sterner, was the rock that held our family together...just like Christ is the "rock of our salvation." My mother took us to church and Sunday school every week. She taught me to cook, to clean, to care for myself, and to take care of my sisters and family.

When we were sick, my mother took care of us. When my mother got sick with cancer, we took care of her just as she taught us to do. She was strong and never wanted to "give up." She wanted to keep living and loving. She was willing to try any treatment or medication that might give her more time or even a cure. She lived life to the fullest until her cancer finally took her life. I miss my mother.

Our parents were hard-working people who sacrificed so much to give us the life of our dreams. I believe that the greatest gift they gave to us was the gift of "faith." They trusted us to endure through all types of troubles. Our parents had a little time to enjoy their three grandchildren, and my only wish is that they could have lived to see their great-grandchild.

We were all very blessed to have such loving and caring parents. I will miss them until I see them again.

Nancy Meck
2012

GIFTS FROM MY FATHER
Kay Schweyer

My father, Robert Jacobs, was my best friend! He gave me so much for which I will always be grateful.

He taught me patience, sensitivity, compassion, a wonderful sense of humor, and of course, lots of kindness. We didn't have much money when I was growing up, but he passed on priceless gifts that shaped who I am today. He came from a very poor household, but he chose to become affiliated with the Boy Scouts and the YM/YWCA in Allentown because his father was absent much of the time. He chose to surround himself with positive role models and then became one himself!

He was warm, understanding, encouraging and showed me the importance of the gift of giving to others. He became a funeral director because one of the men for whom he worked offered to send him to mortuary school if he would return and work for that funeral home. Although it was probably not what he would have chosen if given other choices, he took advantage of this opportunity and really became a compassionate, loving, and kind professional in a very tough industry. Many families decided to choose the funeral home for which he worked only because my father was so kind. He was really "leading by example" from that time forward.

He remained a part of the Boy Scouts of America for over fifty years. He was an Eagle Scout as a young man and then led many scout troops over the years. He really wanted to give young boys what he never was able to get as a child. I remember how touching it was when, at my dad's funeral, a young scout came forward and gave a heartfelt tribute to my father and what he had contributed to this young boy's life. My family felt so much pride for my father's life.

We always had a very strong connection right up to the end of his life. Through his battle with Alzheimer's, I would hold his hand and tell him how much I loved him. I told him how much he had meant to me. I comforted him and told him that I was certain everything would be all right.

It's called "role reversal." I had suddenly become his parent, and he was now my child. Caring for my dad in this way was also preparing me for a career change later in my life that I had no idea would materialize. I now care for elderly people in their homes, and on so many occasions, I go back in my mind to the moments like this with my dad.

Above all, we always had laughter and a wild sense of humor. The memories I have of the "wild and crazy" times we had filled with laughter and love are amazing. One of my passions in life is to visit hospitalized people...especially the elderly people who are so often forgotten...and introduce them to my clown identity: Dr. Gigglefritz. Dad, you would be so proud!

My dad: I miss his soft, gentle smile; I miss his encouraging words; I miss him.

Kay Schweyer

HOLIDAY THOUGHTS, 2004
Sylvia Silvetti Havlish

I t's the second Christmas season without my mother. Fourteen months have passed in somewhat of a blur since her beautiful soul escaped from her cancer-ridden body for the "trip of a lifetime." She had "closed her business" with us here and was ready to see her Lord and to reconnect with my father, my brother, and her beloved grandson. I know in my heart that she is finally free, and for her, this holiday must be pure love and peace at last.

Why, then, am I so very, very sad? Why is this worse than last Christmas?

I should know the answers…as a counselor, with a specialty in bereavement…I SHOULD know…but the words of the textbooks bring no solace to my broken heart.

Loss is a deep wound, and although the process is said to bring healing, this process is much harder than I imagined. I thought I was prepared. My beloved father died…again from a ravaging cancer… nineteen years ago in November. My grief was so deep then that it felt like a wound that might be fatal. But something was different. I know now. I still had my mother.

I was not yet a complete orphan…an orphan alone with no parents. You are probably wondering how old this "lonely child" might be. Would you ever come close to guessing that this "child" is fifty-six years old? I am fifty-six, not six, not even sixteen, but fifty-six…and a mother myself of a twenty-six-year-old child. I find myself counting the losses inside my thoughts...those thoughts that just won't be put aside when I try.

One month after my mother, age ninety, died in our home, my precious only child moved from our home to Philadelphia. He had been living away from home since college but found himself back with us for a much-too-short period before my mother became ill. It was so wonderful to have him with us during her illness...and especially during her dying...but the new job and new apartment had become a part of his life just one month after her death.

I t was like another death to me. Only an hour away, you say? Yes, I know. I am not a "smother mother"...and I am so proud that my son has been independent and totally "his own man" for so many years...but when I take stock of our home today, it feels horribly empty.

Yes, I have a husband. Yes, he tries to understand my crying jags, my pitiful times of mourning popping up in the midst of totally unrelated events. But, it feels very empty, and I feel very much alone in the world.

Counting my blessings has always been a part of my daily existence, with thankfulness part of my daily prayers. My blessings include a career I truly love, more friends and acquaintances than one can count, and a busy life style. But guess what? It isn't enough for me. I want my mommy!

Having her live with us for twelve years is among the greatest of blessings I thank God for each day. But the pain of losing this woman of ninety years, who was going on thirty-five, and who knew me and understood me as no one else ever has or ever could, is just too much right now. I see her empty chair. I find her "grocery lists" stuck in every purse I own. I dissolve in a fit of tears and sobs that must sound to others like I've been physically attacked. Of course, almost all of these attacks are when I am alone at home, in the car, or in the aisle of the local Hallmark store. I hear the first three notes of one of her favorite songs, and I am unable to pretend that I am "fine, thank you."

This past week, the anniversary of a young man's death came again…the beloved son of one of my closest friends…who died in an accident at the age of twenty-two. His mother is one of three close friends I have who have lost their children. I feel at the same time a close kinship with them…and a horrible guilt that I am mourning the passing of parents who were seventy-one and ninety respectively… while my friends must endure a life without seeing their beautiful sons and daughters again on this planet. Somehow I know that if my mom and dad have any way of finding these three children, they will be encouraging and loving them as they did for me during their lives on earth.

I write this to help my hurting soul and to reach out to others who will try to walk through this season of joy and peace on earth with their outward expressions set on "automatic" while they feel the quivering of their broken hearts just below the surface almost twenty-four hours a day. We have formed a bond and have been initiated into a "club" we didn't vote to join. But in this season, I offer up to you the hope that is really the message of this beautiful Christmas season. HOPE…the hope that was born in that manger so many, many years ago…and the hope that He gives to all believers that we will again be reunited in Heaven and will come to a celebration TOGETHER that has no ending and no tears.

Sylvia Silvetti Havlish
December 12, 2004

WE LOSE OUR SPOUSES

In the classic book, *The Prophet*, Kahlil Gibran speaks of marriage:

"You were born together, and together you shall be forevermore. You shall be together when the white wings of death scatter your days. Ay, you shall be together even in the silent memory of God. But let there be spaces in your togetherness, and let the winds of the heavens dance between you."

"Spaces in your togetherness"…good advice during your lifetime…but even more poignant when a marriage ends with the death of one of the partners. The spaces can become overwhelmingly big. The loneliness and emptiness of one's new "role" seem like a terrible punishment to the surviving spouse. As in many types of grief, so many friends and family members are there in the very beginning of one's path of grief, but then they are suddenly gone. Their lives go on as "normal" while the widow or widower is just coming out of the shock and beginning to "wake up" to their new reality. The routine and safety of their former life is changed forever as they see that empty chair at the table, as they wait to hear the familiar footsteps coming in the door, or when they try to answer the constant questions of their children.

There are also the terrible feelings associated with grieving when a marriage has been unhappy, abusive, or in some way, flawed. When such surviving spouses come to my bereavement group, I see the anguish in their eyes as they listen to other widows/widowers extolling the virtues of their deceased spouses. They are usually very quiet until they feel the unconditional acceptance and love of the group members. It is then that they are able to share.

Or…as the Beatles sang on their album, *Abbey Road*…

"And in the end…the love you take…

is equal to the love…you make!"

Every Time the Clock Strikes "11:11"
Paulette Nichols-Kennedy

Peter Lee Nichols was born in Barstow, California, on August 14, 1945. As his mother lay in her hospital bed holding her precious little boy, crowds were cheering in the streets below. The war was over. Pete Nichols was born on "VJ" day…a memorable day…a memorable life.

I met my husband-to-be at a meeting of "The Flying Dutchman Ski Club." We had an immediate connection and very early on realized that we had found in one another a best friend and a true soul mate. Pete graduated from Albright College in Reading, Pennsylvania, where he played baseball, leading the team to a number of state titles with his sharp pitching skills. He eventually played baseball for the Dodgers farm team. He loved baseball and continued to play on various teams throughout his life. The number on his jersey was always "11." The number "11" didn't seem to mean very much at the time, but it is truly incredible how it has grown to mean so much to our family.

Pete and I loved to hike on Hawk Mountain. We couldn't think of a more appropriate place to marry and join our lives as one. On a beautiful spring day in May of 1977, my father walked me down a cedar-lined path among the wild flowers with the sun streaming through the trees. This was our perfect place. We had spent many weekend days eating apples and drinking wine on the North Lookout as we waited for a hawk or maybe even an eagle to fly over us as we lay there staring up at the sky. It almost felt as though we could touch Heaven. We so loved our "special place." As we recited our wedding vows on the South Lookout of Hawk Mountain, two hawks circled overhead.

Our happiness became more complete with the birth of our daughter, Jennifer Kyle Nichols, on January 29, 1979. Little Jenny spent many a spring and summer day and evening watching her daddy play baseball. We enjoyed such a rich and full life together. But it was not to last.

On September 11, 1979, shortly after Jenny was tucked into bed and we had gone to sleep for the night, I was abruptly awakened. The bed was shaking. I flew out of the bed and turned on the light to find my husband shaking uncontrollably. I thought he might be having a seizure. I couldn't arouse him. Did he suffer a stroke? What could have gone wrong? Pete was the picture of health, so full of life. No, please, NO! I ran across the street to wake my neighbors after calling the ambulance. After what seemed to be a lifetime, Pete woke up. He began to thrash around and seemed to be fighting and punching the air. My wonderful neighbors took little "Jenniebird" (as they called her) to their home to allow me to go to the emergency room with my husband. Hours of darkness passed with no answers. Night turned to day. A neurosurgeon entered Pete's hospital room. Pete's parents and I stared at the doctor trying to read his face and praying that the news would be good.

We were told that Pete had suffered a seizure due to pressure on his brain from a "growth" of some kind. He would have to operate the next morning to remove it. The reality of what I was hearing was too much to process.

The next morning, Pete went to the operating room. His family and I and a room full of friends and colleagues waited for some word, any word. We waited for more than twelve hours and still heard nothing. I happened to see my pediatrician walk by and begged him to help me to get some news about my husband. We were told that the doctor would meet us on the third floor in one hour. As we sat waiting, I could feel my heart pounding. I could not believe that any doctor would complete a surgery and allow a family to suffer for hours awaiting news of their loved one's condition.

When the doctor finally met with us, it didn't take long for him to say, "Pete has a grade 4 Astrocytoma multiforme...a deadly brain tumor." I was not a nurse at the time and had no knowledge of the seriousness of this diagnosis. The doctor's next words were, "He has no more than two weeks to a month to live." Pete was terminally ill! What was to be our child's first Christmas was to be his last. Pete's parents walked away together after hearing the news as I sat alone not knowing what to think or what to do.

The surgery was a success! They "got it all"...all except "the music lessons"...some very poor medical humor at a very inappropriate time. Following a full course of radiation therapy, Pete seemed to be confused. He was readmitted to the hospital where we were told, once again, that treatment was futile. I was so angry that they thought they had the right to "play God" and take our hope from us. I didn't, couldn't or wouldn't, believe that my husband was going to die...at least not without a fight.

The day after Christmas, I took Pete to Memorial Sloan-Kettering Cancer Center in New York. After a six-hour wait, we were escorted to Pete's room. Two neurologists conducted intensive assessments along with additional CT scans and MRIs. The following morning I was told they felt he could be helped. He was placed on three different chemotherapeutic medications and had weekly visits to New York for blood work and treatments. It is during a time like this when you find out who your friends really are. Pete's co-workers took turns taking him to New York City for his weekly treatments to allow me to work and be at home with our little girl. We tried to pay them, but no one would take a penny!

Pete was eventually given the closest thing to a clean bill of health that he would get. He returned to work at the Travelers Insurance Company and yes, returned to baseball...this time wearing a specially-made hard hat. During these months we truly felt blessed. We had a renewed appreciation for life and everything around us.

We watched our little girl grow and enjoyed precious family time… although borrowed.

In March of 1982, as we were leaving a restaurant, Pete told me that the street we were crossing was "slanting downhill." He became disoriented. We rushed back to the local hospital. The brain tumor had returned, this time larger than before.

Once again, we traveled to Memorial Sloan-Kettering. This time I couldn't find a place for Jenny and me to stay. The hospital had made arrangements for us at a church. When we arrived, we learned that our room had been given away. On the way back to the hospital, the stroller broke. When we finally reached my husband's room, we were extremely tired. At that time, hospitals had "day rooms" at the end of the unit. There were forty cancer patients on this wing of the hospital. I was so touched when many of them came out to the "day room," pushed couches together, and provided us with blankets and pillows so that we would have a place to stay. They were extremely ill but worried more about our comfort.

Chemotherapy and surgery were not the only things that were happening in that hospital. Laughter filled the rooms and hope was very much alive. I went out and bought decorations and a cake for my husband's roommate to celebrate his fortieth and last birthday. Those people held me up. They were so very ill, and yet they came into my heart leaving footprints—and I would never be the same again. In fact, our little daughter was potty trained in one of the most famous cancer facilities in the world!

A month passed. It was now time to try to accept the inevitable… that Pete would not recover…that he could not live the life he loved so much. I brought him home to 24/7 nursing care. On the morning of April 21, 1982, it was evident that he had but a short time to be with us. He never opened his eyes that day until our daughter was next to him. He reached for her, touched her, and tried to take a last look at the little girl he would leave behind. It was raining that day. When the rain finally stopped, a beautiful rainbow was visible right over our home. Pete's family and I spent hours with him that day into the evening watching as his breathing slowed as he was moving away from us to a place where there is no pain. I don't know what came over me, but I ran to the stereo and played Through the Years by Kenny Rogers. I climbed into bed and held Pete very tightly until he took his last breath. I stayed right there for a long time. On that night the world lost a courageous, kind and compassionate man who was loved by all who knew him. Jenny and I suffered the biggest loss that day.

I awoke the next morning to the sounds of birds chirping. The sun was shining brightly. I remember thinking that this was Pete's favorite kind of day. It didn't seem real.

In the days and months that followed, I was lost. I thanked God for my little "Jenniebird" every single day. She is what kept me focused on living and putting one foot in front of the other. I had no choice. I couldn't just fold up, she needed me. I brought Jenny into my bed each night as I couldn't bear to be alone. This is also when my daughter was introduced to "fast food." I couldn't sit at our dinner table and stare at his empty chair.

One day shortly after Pete's passing, the funeral director came to my door wearing his long black coat. He knocked on the door, and when I answered, he handed me a small brown plastic box. Was this what was left of my beloved husband? My heart ached, but I knew what I had to do. Pete had asked to be cremated and that his ashes go with the sun and the wind from the South Lookout of Hawk Mountain.

On a beautiful spring day, among the wild flowers, with the sun steaming through the trees, I went out to the farthest rock. Our minister was softly praying in the background while John Denver was singing Pete's favorite songs from a small tape player that was set on a rock. There was sun but no wind. I looked up and saw one hawk circling overhead. I tossed Pete's ashes into the air with all my might and sure enough, the wind carried them on their way. I knew in that moment that everything was just as it should be. A profound peace came over me.

Five months after Pete's passing, I entered nursing school. I had seen too much and wanted to give back, to make it easier for anyone who might have to travel a similar path. I kept in touch with the patients and spouses who shared the corridor in Memorial Sloan-Kettering that past March. There is not one of those loving, caring people who are alive today. But their lives had meaning. I know that they appreciated each day that they were given…probably more than those who have had the good fortune not to be touched by tragedy. They live on! Pete lives on!

When "Jenniebird" graduated from Villanova University, one hawk flew over the stadium during the entire ceremony and then disappeared. When Pete's father had open heart surgery, one hawk circled over his home in South Carolina. I have already seen one hawk perched on my deck and also on my mailbox…both times on days when I felt that I really could not handle things very well. I suppose we all believe what we believe. I mentioned the number eleven. Pete's obituary was on page eleven of the newspaper. His last Easter was April 11th. We were married on Hawk Mountain at eleven a.m. When I sat for my Pennsylvania State Board of Nursing exam, I was seated in section 11, row 11, seat 11. When I turned my test paper over, the number "11" was in the corner. Every time I feel melancholy, the number "11" pops up somewhere. Our daughter became engaged in 2011. It just goes on and on. I derive great comfort when I glance at the clock and it says, "11:11!" Hello, Pete, I know you are here with me.

My Eulogy for My Husband, Peter L. Nichols

Pete may have lost the battle, but he won the war. There were too many battles, full of peaks and valleys with many a cross to bear. But Pete was no quitter and fight he did until the final battle began. When his body could no longer endure the battle, I began to fight for him. I became his slow-moving footsteps and his shaky movements as he would fumble trying to accomplish the smallest tasks which were once second nature to him. I shed his tears of sorrow, frustration, anger, pain, desperation, and fear as he lay unable to express himself.

Pete was my strength. He never doubted, and he never gave in to what his mind must have been telling him was reality. He continued to live, laugh, love, and reassure us all time and time again that he was fine.

He pulled me up when I was downhearted so many times. We had a very special understanding between us when words were no longer necessary. One always seemed to know what the other was feeling and knew exactly what to do about it.

I don't need another day to tell Pete how I feel. There is a great deal of comfort and peace knowing that we have said it all.

Despite adversity, Pete Nichols taught me to live life to its fullest and to appreciate every hour of every day. He taught me to persevere and to be independent.

There is a plaque that hangs in my bedroom, one that I gave to my husband during his illness. I don't know the name of the author, but I will never forget the words:

That man is a success
Who has lived well, laughed often and loved much;
Who has gained the respect of intelligent men and the love of children;
Who has filled his niche and accomplished his task;
Who leaves the world better than he found it, whether by an improved poppy,
A perfect poem or a rescued soul;
Who never lacked appreciation of earth's beauty and
Who looked for the best in others and gave the best he had.

I will have a place in my heart for Pete as long as I live, and I know that our very special "rainbow connection" will continue for all the days of my life. Whenever I feel defeated, sad or lonely, all I need do is look at the clock. It will be "11:11" and I will feel comforted once again. Pete is there telling me that everything will be okay.

Paulette Nichols-Kennedy

Sue and Scott Fichter

IN MEMORY OF SCOTT
Sue Fichter

As a bereavement counselor, I have been facilitating two groups each year sponsored by Lutheran Congregational Services. Each group meets for six consecutive Wednesday evenings, and each semester I wonder who God is sending to me at that time. In October of 2011, I had just taken my seat to await the new "class" of people who had joined the ranks of "bereaved" persons. One of the women who entered that night was a lovely young woman who was already dissolved in tears. I greeted her and held her as she sobbed. I wondered who she had lost and how recently her loss had been. I asked and found that she had lost her beloved husband, Scott, less than one month before this class started.

During that class I asked the participants to bring something in that would show their unique relationship with their deceased loved one. On the last night, Sue handed me an envelope with some pictures of herself with Scott...and of her two beautiful daughters with their father. The simple, yet poignant writing that she gave me that night is very powerful. I just knew I wanted her writing to be a part of Moments Like This. Here it is:

May, 1985. Two hearts meet. Friendship turns into love. Two hearts become one.

I have always thanked God for: you, our special bond, our beautiful daughters, Samantha and Shannon, and the wonderful life I live. I am blessed to have you by my side to create twenty-six years of memories. I have watched you become a loving husband, devoted father, dedicated volunteer coach to hundreds of youth, best friend to many, and a committed Miami Dolphins fan.

September 15, 2011. My heart aches for: your presence, your voice, you to hold my hand. But, as our daughters point out to me when we see a beautiful Aqua and Orange colored sky, I know without a doubt that with the help of God, you are by my side forever.

We love you forever!

Sue, Samantha and Shannon XOXO

THE LAST SUMMER
Suzanne Kozy

It was New Year's Day in 2007. My thoughts were positive and happy. "This is going to be a great year...I can feel it in my heart," I thought. I knew that I would be adding a new decade to my life this year with my sixtieth birthday on the way. My youngest granddaughter, Emma, would also celebrate her first birthday on my birthday! She was a wonderful birthday present to me last year. On my birthday in 2007, my family surprised me at work with balloons and flowers followed by a party later that evening. As I cut my cake, I discovered a piece of metal. Horrified, I pulled it out to find the key to a brand new 2007 Pontiac Vibe from my husband. It was the best birthday ever! I told everyone that I was certain this was going to be a great year.

How was I to know that it would be the worst year of my life? My world was about to fall apart, and I would feel as if my life was over.

The journey began in June. Rich was not feeling well and was complaining of pain in his back and chest. He had a severe cough and his lungs hurt. After much convincing, he went to his doctor on June 23, 2007. He was given some muscle relaxers and an anti-inflammatory drug for the pain. When we asked about the cough and chest pain, the doctor replied, "Let's just take one thing at a time." For two weeks Rich took the drugs but was unable to sleep from the tremendous pain.

He returned to the doctor on July 3 and he was sent for x-rays of the left hip and back as well as his lungs. On July 5 he had his yearly colonoscopy and one polyp was removed. After the procedure, he started to have severe constipation along with his increasing pain and sleeplessness. He was told that the pain pills caused the constipation.

We had a family yearly beach trip tradition which Rich never attended, but he told me to go with the family as usual on July 7. By July 10 we still had not heard any results from the x-rays, and Rich went in to his doctor to demand an explanation. He was told he had pneumonia and arthritis and was prescribed more drugs. He kept following the medical instructions but with absolutely no good results. In fact, he was still unable to eliminate the wastes from his body by July 19th. On July 20th, he weighed 139 pounds and had lost 20 pounds. By that time he could not sit or walk without incredible pain.

His pain was so intense that I took him to the emergency room on July 21. After five hours of x-rays and tests, he was given more pain medication and sent home. The next morning he called his doctor and begged him to send him for an MRI of his back. We got the results on the evening of July 24. The news was devastating, and it was the worst day of our lives. We were told that Rich had spinal cancer. It was more than we could take in mentally. Rich told the doctor he could accept that he had cancer, but he could no longer stand this pain. They gave him oxycontin and sent him home again. Rich had an appointment with the oncologist on July 27 which was his 64th birthday.

We remembered that several months before all this pain started, Rich had some blood work which showed that his white blood cell count was elevated. No further tests had been scheduled to determine the reason for this count until the doctors now started to put the pieces of the puzzle together. When they told us the terrible news and his prognosis, I had an anxiety attack and could not believe what I was hearing. Rich tried to comfort and help me. That is when the word "Denial" came into my life in a rush.

I asked our daughter to come to our son's home, and then I told them the sad news. We all hugged each other and cried together for a long time. We decided that we would try to stay strong for Dad and for each other. But on July 28th when our family gathered at our home to finally celebrate Rich's birthday, he was in so much pain that he still could not sit on a chair and could barely walk. He had to lie on the living room floor, and although he had very little appetite, that is where he ate his food. As the days passed, I was feeling so helpless and so angry. "I want my husband back. I want him to be able to sit at the table and eat with me," I cried. "Please, God, help me to do the right thing and help me take care of him."

On August 3, Rich was able to attend a family graduation party with the help of a lidocaine patch on his back. He used crutches, but he was still in agony. When his brother and his family saw Rich's condition, they were both shocked and terribly saddened. My husband's condition kept deteriorating, but I kept telling myself that he would eventually be better.

Then early in the morning of August 8, I was awakened as Rich was having some type of terrible "attack." He couldn't breathe; he was sweating profusely and having chest pains. I was certain it was a heart attack, but after several minutes he was able to calm down and we realized he was having a full-blown anxiety attack…and with good reason. On August 12, he was having another very painful day. He took me by the hand and told me that he was sure the he was "going downhill" rapidly and knew that he was dying. I immediately said, "Don't say that!" Denial was holding on to me.

His pain was so intense the next day that we took him to the hospital again, hoping for some miracle pain medication that would allow him to sit and walk again. They did another MRI.

All I remember are the words, "…cancer everywhere…lungs, bones, liver, throughout his entire body…terminal." Now Rich was comforting me once again. I did not want to believe this, but he had accepted his fate. He promised to fight as hard as he could so that he could get home and "get things in order."

Now our days were going by much too quickly as he started his first radiation treatment on August 14. They seemed to be trying everything including physical therapy, pain patches, and morphine to lessen his pain. They even fitted him with a brace which he was to wear whenever he tried to walk. He hated it. It was so tight he had more difficulty breathing. I kept calling the doctor to get more information and help, but the calls were never returned. I was becoming frustrated and full of fear. He was having radiation every day and developed a rash on his back and legs which "itched like crazy" and caused him more pain. Then, his legs and feet were becoming cold all the time, and he could never get warm.

August 24, 2007 was our 39th Wedding Anniversary. I entered his hospital room and found that they had taken him for another MRI. He was gone for more than three hours, and when he returned, he was so happy that I had waited for him to return. I climbed into bed with him, and he managed to hold me in his arms. It was so hard not to cry. Who would have ever believed that we would spend our 39th anniversary in a hospital room while his condition was getting worse? That night I cried myself to sleep and begged God to make him better. I never felt so lonely or alone before. I had married Rich when I was very young and went directly from my parent's home to our home together.

On August 27 he had his last radiation treatment and started his chemotherapy treatments on August 31. We were taking him back and forth from home to the hospital for these treatments, and we were all under incredible stress. When we talked together, he said that he wanted to get well enough to go back in the woods and hunt mushrooms and shoot horseshoes with is son. He loved spending time in the woods and always said that "his church was being by himself in the woods and communing with God." We spent time watching television together and doing crossword puzzles. We would hold each other and stay as close as possible until the pain would require Rich to move. My heart was breaking for him as I watched the love of my life just diminishing before our eyes. The day he had chemo they weighed him, and he was down to 120 pounds and looked like "skin and bones."

On September 3, Labor Day, I found him on the floor of the bathroom. He said he crawled into the room knowing he had diarrhea and just couldn't make it up on to the toilet. The next morning the ambulance took him to the hospital again. My son and daughter stayed with me in his room the rest of the day and night. We were all devastated watching him in this weakened condition. All he wanted to do was go home, but we knew that we could never give him the care he needed. The decision was made to move my beloved Rich to the hospice unit in Allentown.

The first thing the nurse said to me when I entered the hospice floor was "What funeral director do you want to use?" I still believed that he could get well, and we would bring him home. I was in total shock. However, as they settled him in to his new room, they said they wanted to bathe him and give him a shave. He said that he wanted me to do it, but they told him that I could do it the next day. I told him I loved him, and he told me he loved me, too.

Little did I know that these words would be the last we would ever exchange.

When we came in the next morning, he looked clean, shampooed and shaved. He was sleeping and snoring peacefully. Suddenly the priest entered the room to give him the last rites. Once again, I was in total denial. I sat in the room, and we all cried. Then at noon, he awakened and asked for a Coke! My daughter got one and gave him some ice cream. She asked him what he thought of his room, and he said, "It's ugly!" Good old Rich! He was always honest. Then he went back to sleep, and I sat rubbing his head and holding his hand. We could feel the love in that room. By the morning of September 7, he was in a coma, and by his facial expressions we knew he was in pain. We all kept talking to him and reassuring him that we would all be okay. The nurses told us that the last sense to "go" is hearing. He was receiving morphine from an intravenous drip and upping the dose as he continued to struggle. My son brought in one of his Dad's favorite CDs by Jack Scott and played it in the room. As soon as it started playing, Rich started to relax and looked calm. When the CD was over, Rich opened his eyes and looked at the three of us standing right next to him. A tear rolled down his cheek as he closed his eyes for the last time. I knew that it was his way of saying goodbye to us. We put the music back on, and the nurse came in to tell us that there was now no heartbeat in his arms or legs—and that it wouldn't be long before he was gone. At 7:40 p.m., the nurse told us he was gone. I screamed and laid on top of him and wanted the nurse to turn the oxygen back on. It seemed that my life had completely fallen apart in that instant. We stayed with him until nine p.m. and by then I knew that he was with God as he looked so serene and peaceful. His battle was over.

I went through the funeral and the preparations in a "blur" of memories and sadness. We sorted pictures for a DVD and chose his favorite songs to play with the pictures. The songs we picked out were The Dance by Garth Brooks, Go Rest High on that Mountain by Vince Gill and Remember When by Allen Jackson. When the day came for me to see him at the funeral home and hear the DVD, I really "lost it" and the reality hit me. He is really gone. He is not coming back. Over 200 people came to honor him, and their presence meant so much to my family and me.

The next two weeks were a frightening combination of making tough choices, getting things in order, and trying to make sense of my new life. I started going to a bereavement support group and that is where I met Sylvia Havlish, the counselor facilitating the group. There were only four of us in the group, and we were able to share our stories of grief with each other for the next six Wednesday evenings. It was so helpful to be with people who really understand where you are as they are at the same place. I am thankful for Sylvia and for the friends I made in that group.

I pray each day that God will allow me to keep going forward, and I talk to Rich each day, too.

As the months progressed, I attended the bereavement group again the next semester, and this time found that I knew I had moved on slowly. I found myself able to help some of the newer members of this club we didn't vote to join. I started to find my inner strength and found that I was able to do many of the things that I never thought I could do. I found that most people are willing to lend a hand to help out. I maintained the friendships of the people in our bereavement groups, and then Sylvia suggested that I join a weekly morning group she has that is "ongoing" and not just for bereaved people. It is called "Getting Unstuck," and I realize that this incredible group of women is exactly where I needed to be. Sylvia has been my "guardian angel," sister, mentor, and friend. I am so grateful for her and for the women in my group and don't really know where I would be if not for their love and support.

It is now four years and four months since I lost my husband, and I never thought I would ever say this, but I love my life again. I am so happy, and I think it is because I have my "sisters" from our group, Sylvia, my children and grandchildren, and especially, Dave. YES! Two years ago he became part of my life, and I thank God every day that He sent him to me.

He called me two years ago to see how I was doing, and I discovered that his wife had passed away just one month after my beloved husband had died. He also told me that we are "neighbors" on the same country road. I realized that forty-five years ago in high school I had a crush on him. I knew him then, but we were both extremely shy. He never knew how I felt back then, but when he called, we found we had so much in common and talked easily. It is truly a "small world," and I thank God that His timing is so good. I would have never been ready to even talk to anyone else before that much time had passed. I told Sylvia then that I thought I was really beginning to "get unstuck" and felt ready to live again and be happy. As Sylvia always tells us, healing and happiness is a choice! She was right. Life can get better again if you are willing to give it time and decide to live again.

Suzanne Kozy   January 2012

Loretta Micucci Gatto "A Long Journey on the Path of Grief"
Phillip Gatto

My beautiful wife, Loretta, was diagnosed with terminal Hodgkin's Disease in 1966, shortly after our daughter, Dawn, was born. She was given six months to live. We had a two year old son and were living in Maryland with no family near us for support. I was just twenty-four years old, struggling to make the mortgage payments, and our future suddenly looked very bleak.

Loretta was admitted into an experimental cancer treatment program at the National Institute of Health (NIH) in Washington, D.C. Although the treatments "saved" her life at that time, it set a tone for many, many years to come. She would have repeated bouts of Hodgkin's for the next thirty-six years. But despite all of this, we were determined to have a good family life together. We did many things that "normal" healthy families did, but we had a "sadness" cloud hanging over our heads...and in our hearts.

Loretta's health was moving along as well as expected until 1992. Then, her lungs started to fail because of the massive radiation treatments she had undergone in the "experimental years" of her disease. Radiation was much stronger in those days compared to the "short wave" radiation of today. As I look back, I think these episodes were the beginning of her "downward spiral."

From 1992 to 1995 she traveled between Johns Hopkins Medical Center in Baltimore, NIH, and the Mayo Clinic desperately trying to find a way to make her "comfortable." Loretta was a fighter, and I loved her spirit and attitude. In 1996 her doctors discovered that her condition would not improve as she had only one full lung and half of the other one able to work. In 1997, she lost thirty percent of her "good lung" and her daily life became a struggle.

She wanted to work to keep her mind focused on something positive and to help with our huge medical bills. As I look back, I believe that her work life kept her moving forward mentally by focusing on other people and things. Loretta was a beautiful, bright, and loving woman. Everyone loved her. We loved each other very much, but I could feel the situation and stress taking a toll on me also. I had to be strong for her, for the children, and to help her keep her sanity. She lost her mother to cancer in 1982 and then her father to a heart attack in 1986. This loss also put a terrible strain on her, both emotionally and physically.

In 1998 the doctors' diagnosed her "illness" as "bronchiectasis." Loretta contracted pneumonia and recovered but had to start using oxygen on a daily basis. We took a trip to Disney World in May of 2001, and that was the last "good time" we had before the illness really started to take her away.

Her oxygen level had to be increased greatly, and she had to use a nebulizer four times a day just to clear her air passage. In January, 2002, she began a cycle of being hospitalized for eight days, then home for eight days. All emergency trips to the hospital were by ambulance. On April 15, 2002, she was placed in a critical care facility. Loretta died on April 26, 2002. It was a very dark day for us.

It is of some comfort to us that Loretta's volunteering for experimental treatment at NIH ultimately paved the way for the successful treatment of Hodgkin's Disease. Her treatments did give us many more years together, although they were very difficult years for everyone in the family. But, as those of us on the "path of grief" agree, the time we have is never enough.

Philip Gatto   January, 2012

"Til Death Do Us Part"
Teal Rhudy

The date was November 4, 2009…a beautiful fall day. The sun was shining, leaves had turned to autumn colors, and the temperature was typical for that time of the year. My day started out as a "normal" day and then something went terribly wrong. It was the day that my life would be changed forever.

I was working at an animal hospital and doing my job as usual when one of the receptionists came to the treatment area and whispered to me that a detective was there to speak with me. My mind automatically went to my beloved husband, Chris. What happened? Was he in trouble? Is he okay?

As soon as I entered the room where the detective was waiting, I sensed that something was terribly wrong. He couldn't give me the "details" although I believe he did have them. He told me to grab my purse and come with him. He was driving me to the hospital. From that moment on, my heart started to pound in my chest. On the way to the hospital, the detective tried to talk with me, but I couldn't think or talk. I just wanted to get to Chris.

As I entered the hospital emergency department, I was rushed into a back room, and there I saw Chris' dad. He met my eyes and told me that he had received a call to come to the hospital immediately. Both of us were Chris' emergency contacts at his job. The doctor came into the secluded room and explained to us in medical terminology that Chris was in a "work accident," his heart couldn't handle it, and he did not survive. At that moment in time, I heard the words that no young bride could ever imagine hearing. I thought, "No! It's not possible. He's only twenty-six years old, healthy and vibrant, and we were not even married for one year...NO! This is not possible." The screaming, tears and shock all rushed over me. My heart felt as if it was pierced and taken out of my body. I was not whole without my Chris.

Friends and family came to the hospital. I remember calling the people who loved me and Chris the most. I wanted them to be near me. I didn't know why, but I needed their presence, their support. Although many people started to arrive, only Chris' parents, my parents, and me were permitted to see Chris. At that time, I just couldn't spend any time with his body...it was just too difficult for me. When I look back, however, I am so glad that I did get to spend even a little time with him one more time...even in his condition.

I think that from that time on I just sat in the dark, secluded room staring at the floor. I couldn't seem to "wrap my head around" this situation. This morning I was a happy married young woman with her entire life ahead of her. Now, I don't have my Chris. I remember the many friends and family who were there expressing the same feelings. I remember my mother pulling my hair back as I vomited into a trash can. I had to get out of that hospital.

My friends and family members came to my sister's house with me. I asked my Dad to go to our home and pick up our dog, Phoebe. When I saw her, I really started to break down. That was to be the first night in seven years that I didn't have Chris lying next to me in bed. I grabbed one of his sweatshirts and cried myself to sleep.

I started looking back. I remembered the first time I ever saw Chris. I was fifteen years old, and he was showing off his Ford Explorer to his friends. I couldn't stop staring at him. He had such an energy about him. He was magnetic...and had so much passion in life. I know that part of his passion was for me as we started dating after our first meeting. Chris and I were "crazy" for each other, and it was actually overwhelming. He could look into my eyes and take my breath away. His smile, his touch, his kisses were all I cared about, but because of our young ages, the timing just wasn't right then.

After a few years, I was eighteen and Chris was nineteen when I attended a party at his Dad's home. We were inseparable after that night. The time we shared together always felt special whether it was just watching television together or hiking the Appalachian Trail together. Our time together was sacred. It was as if all we ever wanted was to be together. Now I understand why: our time together was going to be too short.

Our wedding day was magical. Although we didn't have a formal wedding, it couldn't have been better. We were married by a justice of the peace in the courthouse. I borrowed an antique dress from my mother, and I bought Chris a suit. He looked so handsome. We each came to the courthouse with our separate families, and when I saw Chris walking towards us, he had a smile that melted my heart.

We stood in front of the judge, and she asked me to say my vows. I did so without hesitation. Then she turned to Chris. Before she could finish what she was saying, he blurted out, "I do, I do!" We all laughed at his eagerness to become my husband! I will never forget that moment.

And now the present came rushing back to me. The next couple of days after his death continued to be horrible. I had to plan his funeral and make decisions that most twenty-four year old women never have to do. I just kept going over and over in my thoughts how this tragedy could have happened. My heart still felt as if there was a sharp stabbing pain and the void will be there forever.

The day of Chris' funeral was another beautiful fall day. I looked outside, and nothing had changed. The sun was shining, the weather was warm for fall, and the leaves turned to all sorts of beautiful colors. Just like the day my life changed forever when I learned of his death…but now I was going to say goodbye to him…to the person I had given my entire heart to just less than a year earlier.

It has now been over two years since Chris passed away, and I can tell you that it never gets easier. The pain of loss is always with me, and half of my heart is still gone. But there is hope. I have learned that there is a light at the end of this tunnel, and I need all the people who love me to keep reminding me that there is light. I wake up each morning a whisper a prayer of gratitude for the time I had with Chris and for the fact that I am here and trying to live each day to the fullest.

Losing Chris made me grow up so fast and realize more about life and death than I would have imagined. I know that my relationship with Chris is a huge part of the woman who I am today, and he has inspired me to live life.

I recently moved to Arizona and have met and become engaged to an amazing man who supports me no matter if it is a good day or not. I found that I had to keep holding on to hope, even when it is "miniscule" and it will definitely surprise you when you least expect it.

Teal Rhudy
January, 2012

SIGNS OF TENDER LOVE
Wanda Fretz

In the fall of 2010, my husband Jay, age fifty-two, had health issues that resulted in subsequent visits to the local emergency room. He was a two-time kidney transplant recipient, the first at age twenty-six from a living donor, his father, and the second a cadaveric eleven years later. His life from transplantation on consisted of a handful of pills every morning and evening with an unending list of serious possible side effects. Regardless of that fact, he managed to retain an amazing zest for life and took good care of himself with daily exercise, maintaining a healthy diet, and regularly scheduled doctor visits.

My world was jolted with news of the first impending transplant. Our two sons were five and three-years old at the time. Several of Jay's relatives on the maternal side had inherited a kidney disease known as Alport Syndrome. My thought was that someday both of our sons would be faced with the same prognosis. Fortunately, a visit to the Hospital of the University of Pennsylvania (HUP) proved that our boys would be free of the disease. A weight was lifted from my shoulders with that news. I knew that my constant and heartfelt prayers were being answered. The Lord had smiled down on my family, and together with Jay's positive attitude, I felt certain he would be alright. One month past his first transplant, he experienced a major rejection episode. So back to HUP and after three grueling weeks, everything seemed to have stabilized. Jay could come home, and eventually, it was life back to "normal". The second transplant was yet another blow, but for a number of reasons, it was a much easier transition mentally and physically.

Fast forward to the fall of 2010. Life had been good to us. We had a comfortable lifestyle and after thirty-two years of marriage, we were still in love, best of friends and soul mates. Our children, Jared and Christian, were happy with their fiancés and lives. Jared and Kelly had set their wedding date, April 30, 2011, in Pittsburgh. Jay and I had a fantastic group of friends and loved ones. So just when we thought things should go on like this into our twilight years, we were thrown a nasty curve ball! In the spring of 2011 after the third trip to the ER in several months, the gastroenterologist determined that Jay was in need of an endoscopy even though his last one was just slightly over a year ago. We awaited the results.

I remember the exact moment my grief journey began. It was a Tuesday, I assumed like many others, when Jay called to tell me he would be home for lunch. He walked in the door as I was preparing our lunch, stood beside me, and said, "Look at me," and as my eyes met his, he said, "We have cancer." I immediately started crying, and we embraced. He then held my face in his gentle yet strong, beautiful hands and without a tear in his eyes told me it would be alright. Jay was always so confident and reassuring, just two of his many wonderful personality traits that enveloped me with a sense of security and warmth. I needed to be strong for him even though I was worried and afraid like no other time in my life.

As I tried to catch my breath, we continued on this unwanted path. Jay needed to have further medical tests to determine the extent of this cruel, invasive disease. Our appointment with the surgeon revealed that Jay's cancer seemed to be limited to his stomach and perhaps the transverse colon. The surgery would be similar to a gastric bypass in that his stomach would be removed but also a portion of the transverse colon as well His eating habits would change a bit as he would be consuming small amounts of food often. He was perfectly okay with that as he was no stranger to challenge and adversity. He said to the doctor, "Let's get this done. I have a wedding to go to!" As a manager of a local BMW Dealership, his "take charge" persona kicked into high gear.

The surgery was scheduled for April 14th, just two weeks before the wedding. We were very grateful to the doctor for fitting him into his surgical schedule so quickly. With my husband's health history and BMW position, he had lots of connections at the hospital and a lot of people pulling for him! I decided to put my real estate license in escrow so I could be there for Jay full time.

A friend suggested utilizing the "Caring Bridge" website in order to keep people informed and eliminate repetitious conversations. I began the first of 21 journal entries on April 13th and emailed the notification of the website to a rather large list of friends, family, and business associates who would want to be kept in the loop. The word spread deep and wide of Jay's impending surgery. The Guest Book entries poured in with words of love and encouragement.

There was a calm sensation permeating the pre-surgical room as our sons, their fiancés, and our two very close friends sat with us awaiting the surgery. Jay was responsible for that feeling. The surgeon came in to answer our questions. I wanted to know how the doctor was feeling and also asked how long the surgery might take. His response was "Great. It will take about three hours. Do you want me to hurry?" We all laughed at his comment and said "NO!" Everyone gave Jay their love, hugs, kisses, and off they went to the waiting room. I spent a few extra minutes with him doing the same. His strength and courage was amazing.

After about three hours, I got a call from a surgical nurse telling me that they removed the tumor and that they were still in surgery. I was a little confused because I didn't recall hearing anything about a tumor at any of our appointments. But I brushed it off thinking that it might just be assumed when talking about cancer. My brother, Hugh, who happens to be a recovery room nurse, popped his head out into the waiting room to see how we were doing and to say they were still in surgery. I told him about the call, and he really didn't have a response. Little did I know that he was not in a position to tell me what was happening.

Five hours passed. I was getting a bit concerned but tried to tell myself that perhaps the doctors had to get to another surgery before speaking to us or maybe started a little later than expected. I had resolved to remain positive or ignorant, or possibly both!

Shortly thereafter, we were taken to a consultation room to speak to the surgeons. Upon seeing the grave expressions on their faces, my heart sank to my stomach. The cancer was more extensive than originally thought. It was as if someone threw a handful of seeds and scattered them among his organs. The surgeon had a pretty good read on Jay and decided to do surgically what he would have wanted done to him had he been in that position. He told us that a lot of other surgeons would have closed him right back up after seeing his situation. He was actually amazed that Jay could even get food down at all. So he was very aggressive and removed his entire stomach, spleen, transverse colon, a portion of his pancreas, and part of the colon. I was shattered to the core in learning that news. My cries were guttural as my boys, trying to remain strong, held on to me from either side. The very real thought of losing my husband hung in the balance. All I knew was that I needed to hang on tight because this was going to be a horribly rough time.

Jay was taken to ICU where he received outstanding care and occupied a room at the end of the long hallway for nineteen days. I was astounded that the surgeon made it a priority to contact me daily with an update after rounds. He would remind me that there will be bumps in the road during these trying times. As I reflect on it today, he knew what our future would be, but I had to keep hope in my heart. Jay was heavily sedated and on a ventilator during that time. In the first week alone, he had two additional surgeries. It was a roller coaster ride as the ups and downs were extreme. Things in ICU can change at any given moment, and they certainly did! One instant they were talking about removing him from the ventilator, and the next they would tell me he wasn't ready. Jay's nephrologist and good friend was leaving on a month-long motorcycle trip. Before leaving he told me at some point I may have to make some hard decision as to when enough is enough. He gave me a short list of people I could count on in ICU while he was gone. I was grateful for the friendship he and my husband shared but also how he cared for me.

I honestly don't know how I remained hopeful, but we had an army of loving, caring individuals who were there for us constantly. My sister, Audrey, and my neighbor, Izzie, called every day and went above and beyond in supporting me. They were at my beck and call at all hours of the day and night. Jay's sister, Gwen, with whom he had such a close, tender relationship, was with us on every day off. She and I continue to be a source of strength for each other. I don't think they will ever be able to comprehend the enormity of what their nurturing has done for me. Delicious meals were being provided by friends and church members every weekend. I kept thinking that even in the face of this horrific journey we were truly blessed.

Sadly, the wedding took place without Jay by my side. That just whittled away at my shattered heart even more. Izzie accompanied me for this lovely occasion and our relatives, John & Sue, insisted that we ride to Pittsburgh with them. I had arranged to "Skype" the wedding and for our terrific friends to be with Jay in the event that he would be conscious. Jay never knew the wedding took place or the extent of his surgery until they finally removed the ventilator and reduced the sedative about a week later. His response was that he was glad the wedding wasn't postponed, and he was grateful for all of the doctor's efforts! His gentle acceptance was astounding to me.

He was transported up to a regular room. I remember being a bit joyful as it was a step in the right direction. Perhaps we could beat this. We had an appointment scheduled with the oncologist to meet with us in Jay's room. Apparently his word for the day was "unfortunately." If he used it once, he used it fifty times. "Unfortunately the type of cancer you have doesn't respond to this type of treatment. Unfortunately you need to gain weight in order to have chemo. Unfortunately...unfortunately...unfortunately..."

I decided that he was not the right oncologist for us, and unfortunately for him, he didn't know my husband's determination. We were not ready to give up this battle.

As Jay began eating and taking physical therapy, his strength was returning. His kind spirit earned him many additional friends with the fourth floor staff. He always thanked the doctors, nurses, and techs for taking care of him, as did the boys and I. Finally, the Friday of Memorial Day weekend, Jay was discharged, and we began having visiting nurses teach me how to care for him. I have never had any formal training, and quite frankly I was uneasy about having Jay's life in my hands. His case was complicated, but he had such faith in my abilities and really wanted to be home. That Saturday night, Jay had a reflux episode that aspirated into his lungs resulting in a touch of pneumonia. He had discomfort in the esophagus with eating and drinking so he was becoming weak and dehydrated. I sobbed when I told him that I couldn't take care of him at home and that I had to take him back to the hospital. It broke my already broken heart even more!

Jay spent a few days in ICU again and was moved back up to be cared for by his friends on the fourth floor. As much as they had grown to care deeply for him, the staff naturally hated to see him come back. We continued to get slammed and battered with one problem after the next. The difficulties, setbacks, and challenges that his body underwent were horrifying, and yet his spirit remained intact. We reached a point where Jay would vomit every hour. The doctors tried to find a remedy, but nothing seemed to be working. We then decided to get OACIS (Optimizing Advanced Complex Illness Support) on board. They knew of a combination of drugs used to combat nausea that had not yet been tried on Jay. Thankfully, it was the cure! However, Jay's weight had declined steadily, and there was no way he could withstand chemotherapy. But he was able to come back home for the Fourth of July weekend. It was then that we got Hospice involved.

I was filled with anxiety and felt frightened at the idea of caring for Jay since his last stay at the hospital resulted in more advanced care. He was really pushing to get home, and there was no way I would stand in his way. I hoped and prayed that I could do everything that needed to be done. Luckily, we had the most outstanding hospice nurse, Marci. We all formed an immediate bond, and she taught me what I needed to do and promised that hospice wouldn't abandon me/us.

I took a really deep breath and dove in! I learned how to change ostomy bags, deal with feeding and drainage tubes, tend to bedsores, keep up every four hours with the anti-nausea shots and administer his other necessary drugs. Scattered among these things were emergency room visits and doctor visits. Sleeping through the night was no longer an option. I developed a good system and had my weekly conversation with the infusion pharmacy regarding what I would need for the next delivery. One of the pharmacists commented that I was asked to do more than they ask of anyone else. He said that Jay was a very special and well-loved man in the community. All this is to say that he was definitely a very complex case!

Our weeks were not only filled with regularly scheduled visits from our hospice nurse, occupational therapist, and social worker but also friends, relatives, and co-workers who wanted to stop by. As wonderful as it was, our home became a revolving door and was rather exhausting for both Jay and me. I found myself waiting on guests as well as my ill husband. So we called upon some awesome friends, Mark and Diane, to ask them to host a party where people could see us and talk with Jay. That way we could relax and leave when Jay felt it was necessary. Upon leaving, Jay said with the greatest sincerity, "I had the most awesome time!" My soul jumped with joy! We also decided to schedule a trip to the dealership where he could get to see all of his co-workers. It was there that I had the opportunity to meet the most remarkable woman, Sandi, a business associate of Jay's and now a friend of mine. She is an extraordinary writer and paid such an incredible tribute to Jay and my family. She was yet another gift along this journey.

Weekends were typically reserved for our children and possibly a few other family members and dear friends. We would plan special events for all of us to look forward to. One weekend was a Mexican theme with Maya's homemade guacamole and margaritas. Another was a pool party with a blow up kiddy pool. We made the most of the time that we had together.

Jay decided to try holistic medicine. We made some changes in his diet but he really couldn't eat very much. Because of that fact, every night he needed to be hooked up to TPN, liquid nourishment containing a lot of dextrose. We then needed to keep track of his blood sugar and give him insulin shots.

Jared and Christian learned to do many of the things that I did. Nothing was too much for them to do in order to help their father or me. They called every day that they were not able to be with us. The love and care they showed for Jay was a treasure to behold. We often wondered how we got so lucky to have such tremendous sons! Christian's job afforded him the ability to spend more time here.

Jay made some obvious improvements during his time at home. But after two months, he was beginning to decline. He was having trouble getting out of his chair without help. He was sleeping a lot. We had a hospital bed in our bedroom which was basically only used to change his bags, but it was getting to the point where he would need to sleep in the hospital bed.

Our sons were in again the first weekend in September. Jared and Kelly left for home September 5th. Maya left early the morning of the 6th, and Christian decided to stay. That day we realized that Jay was showing all the signs of leaving this earth very soon. So we called Jared to let him know of his Dad's condition. He was ready to get on the road at 9:30 that evening, but there was a bad storm brewing and I didn't want to worry about him on the road. So I asked him to wait until the morning. No one realized how fast it would happen. Jay was restless during the night. His breathing was labored and irregular, but I made sure he was as comfortable as possible. I put a rocker by the hospital bed and lay against his arm. I woke Christian from his sleep to let him know that it wouldn't be long so he could spend some time with him before he passed. He took his last breath at 5:15 a.m. Wednesday, September 7th, 2011 at the all-too-young age of fifty-three with Christian and me by his side.

I was so fearful of that moment. But the transition seemed fairly easy for him; he had a soft landing. I had hoped that I could give him that as he wanted to die at home. About a half hour before he died, I told him "I love you very much, we love you, we will miss you but we'll be alright." I gave him permission to go. Although it was necessary, it was one of the hardest things to do. I am so grateful to have been with him for his last breath. I couldn't imagine not being there for him.

I called hospice, and they took care of some arrangements. After Jared arrived that morning, we all hugged and cried together, our first act as a family without Jay. Oh, how we would miss him! I then made the necessary calls to relatives and friends to see Jay before they took his body away. He wanted to be cremated. The Memorial service was held on September 16th, 2011.

Jay has given me so many signs. The first was four days after his death. Christian and Maya were in the kitchen, and I was on the computer in my office. The ceiling light is slightly behind where I sit, and suddenly, I noticed a shadow and felt warmth across my shoulders for about two seconds. I turned thinking Christian came in the room without me hearing him, but no one was there. I said, "You're here, aren't you?" At which point, Christian came into the room and asked me what I said. I told him "Your Dad was just here!" What a spectacular feeling and such a comfort to me!

A few days after the Memorial service, I awoke in the middle of the night to see Jay standing five feet from the edge of our bed. He looked beautiful and healthy, but rather serious. I blinked my eyes, and he was gone. When I told my sister-in-law Gwen about it and how he looked, she commented, "That's because he was so concerned about you!"

One day I decided to blow the leaves with the backpack blower.

Jay had shown me how to use it in the past. I made sure there was gas in it, but I had trouble getting it started. After about ten minutes, I became very frustrated. I looked up in the sky and said "Jay, can you help me out please?" The next pull, it started. I said, "Thanks Jay!"

Christmas Day was a difficult day filled with anxiety for me. For the last 38 years, I spent that day with Jay. Jared, Kelly, Christian, and I exchanged our gifts in the morning. Jay's sister and her husband stopped by at noon to spend some time with us. I wasn't finished getting ready when I heard them come to the door. As I entered the family room, they all had a surprised look on their faces. The gas fireplace was off, and at that split second, it turned on. It was not on a timer or set to go on at a certain room temperature, and the batteries in the remote were dead. We knew that was Jay bringing his light and warmth into the room for all of us who love and miss him so dearly!

Later in the day, more family and friends kept us company. But even with a houseful of people, I felt so alone. At one point I noticed the most gorgeous sunset. Jay would always call me if we weren't together to share a sunset with him, and I would do the same. So I went outside by myself and stood in the driveway for about five minutes enjoying the magnificence and solitude. The tears flowed like a waterfall. The signs he gave me could not have been any clearer.

Most recently, a friend told me about pennies she got from her father after he died. I informed her that I was hoping to get a penny. I relayed the story to my boys and that it means an angel from heaven is missing you. Two days later on a Saturday evening, Jared and I were getting ready to go to a party. I went into the coat closet searching for a wine carrier, and as I pulled it out, I heard something drop on the floor. Then I saw it and exclaimed, "Oh,my gosh!" Jared came running. I pointed at the penny, and we both laughed and hugged. I said, "Hi Jay!" I understand that sometimes the penny has some significance. The date on this particular penny is the same year as Jay's second transplant at which time Jared offered his Dad one of his kidneys! Within a few days, several other friends and relatives also received pennies! It brings a smile to our faces along with our tears.

Our family's biggest joy on the horizon is the upcoming birth of our first grandchild. Jay so much wanted a grandchild, and although he left us before finding out this news, I know he is celebrating in heaven.

I have run the full gamut of emotions this past year and struggle to think of one that I haven't yet experienced. Since Jay is gone, I have so much time to reflect on what we went through. Sometimes I play it back in my head and think, "If only I would have done...things might be different!" So there is guilt, real or imagined. However, a very wise woman told me, "You did the best you could at the time." I believe I did.

I feel as though I have aged greatly on this journey, but I have also gained so much wisdom. I remain indebted to the many people who have cradled me and held me up in their loving, caring arms. Their gift to me and my boys is miraculous. I find myself understanding that this is all a part of life, and everyone will experience grief in varying degrees. It is an extremely personal passage, and there are a lot of helpful resources that can be researched.

As I look back at the memorial service, I am amazed at how well the boys and I handled it all. We held our heads high as we remained optimistic, strong, and grateful to the multitude of people who honored this special man's life. I am positive that Jay gave us that strength, and I know he was proud! Jay just knew how to "BE." He knew how to be an excellent husband with such a selfless love, one that I never thought I would find. He knew how to be a terrific father as our boys are a testament to that fact. He knew how to be a wonderful son, in-law, friend, co-worker, man. Jay taught us how to live but also how to die. I recall his words to me one day when he realized that his journey here on earth was coming to an end. He said, "I don't know how to do this. I don't know how to die." But he did know and lived the end of his life with such courage and grace. The human spirit is capable of so much as evidenced so richly by Jay's story.

To Jay:

I will forever toast you and keep you in my heart. Rest in peace, my love; you did so much on this earth and touched so many lives. Thank you for making this chapter of our lives so exceptional. I was honored to be your wife. We were perfect for each other. Thank you also for your many signs to me from heaven as it has given me so much comfort and the will to go on without you. I will be with you again, and it will be an awesome reunion!

Wanda Fretz
January 2012

"Go to the End... See Darkness...Step Out Anyway"
Doreen Pavinski

JANUARY, 2008. I started that year with great expectations. After all, it was a new year and full of new possibilities. So with my desire, expectations and feeling great about life, I began to set some goals, work with possibilities, and live my life as I have done on a daily basis. But that January, things would be different.

My mother died on January 7, and then unbelievably, my devoted husband died on January 15.

It just didn't seem real. I don't know how to put into words what I was feeling during those days. I think I went through the motions of two funerals...perhaps in a fog.

Throughout the last four years, I have felt many different emotions at each stage I walk through the path of grief. I never felt anger. My faith is very strong, and it is very different from being "religious." One day I heard someone define faith as this: "Go to the end, see darkness, step out anyway." That is it. I believe that as we go through tough times in our lives, it is your faith that finally carries you to begin living again.

The memories of my mother and my husband seem to become stronger as I age and go through my life. I know in my heart that they would want me to live. We are "among the living" even when we walk through this valley of death. When I think of my mother, I know that she was my "rock" with her wisdom, her encouragement, and her faith. I learned how to cook from my mom and remember seeing her go to the refrigerator when I knew we didn't have a lot there, and she would emerge with a meal!

When I think of my precious husband, I remember that he always told me that we gave our children solid roots and solid values. He said that I should learn to trust their decisions. Today as I see them mature, I know that he was right.

I believe that by practicing what you have learned from your loved ones, you are honoring them. I cherish all the memories and the lessons I have from my life with my mother and my husband.

Many of you who are reading this may wonder how I started to make the transition from just going over the "would haves," "should haves," and the "what ifs" to actually living intentionally again. Here's my advice: instead of just thinking about starting again, do it! Start with gratitude for the time you did have them. Be grateful each morning for the fact that YOU are still here and alive. Then, make a list of the things you want to do with the rest of your life. Make that "dash" between your birth date and your date of death one that will stand out. You are passing on a legacy of who you are and how you handled life.

When you don't know where to begin to heal, just look around and be grateful.

Doreen Pavinski
January, 2012

WE LOSE OUR CHILDREN

When I was a child, my mother and father read to us all the time. Both of my parents loved poetry and had memorized many poems when they were children. I would be spellbound as they repeated wonderful poems that meant so much to them. But the memory I have that can still start my tears rolling down my face is the one of my mother reciting this incredible poem by Eugene Field about the death of his little boy.

LITTLE BOY BLUE
By Eugene Field (1850-1895)

The little toy dog is covered with dust,
But sturdy and stanch he stands;
And the little toy soldier is red with rust,
And his musket moulds in his hands.
Time was when the little toy dog was new,
And the soldier was passing fair;
And that was the time when our Little Boy Blue
Kissed them and put them there.
"Now, don't you go till I come," he said,
"And don't you make any noise!"
So, toddling off to his trundle-bed,
He dreamt of the pretty toys;
And, as he was dreaming, an angel song
Awakened our Little Boy Blue...
Oh! The years are many, the years are long,
But the little toy friends are true!

Ay, faithful to Little Boy Blue they stand,
Each in the same old place...
Awaiting the touch of a little hand,
The smile of a little face;
And they wonder, as waiting the long years through
In the dust of that little chair,
What has become of our Little Boy Blue,
Since he kissed them and put them there.

People always ask me how I can be a bereavement counselor... and then they add, "I could never counsel anyone who lost a child." My father used to say when a young relative would pass away, "If any of my children die, you might as well just open the grave next to theirs and put me in it. I couldn't survive that loss." I didn't realize the weight of his words until I gave birth to my son, Christopher. I know that every parent knows the feeling.

But the brave parents who here share their profound stories of grieving their children's deaths will start to unlock the mystery of how they find the strength to go on. I consider it one of the greatest gifts that these beautiful people can share with the world. They have proven to me that the words of Kahlil Gibran in his book, *The Prophet*, speak the truth we all hope we don't have to learn.

SPEAK TO US OF CHILDREN

Kahlil Gibran

And a woman who held a babe against her bosom said,
"Speak to us of Children."
And he said:
Your children are not your children.
They are the sons and daughter of Life's longing for itself.
They come through you but not from you,
And though they are with you yet they belong not to you.
You may give them your love but not your thoughts,
For they have their own thoughts.
You may house their bodies but not their souls,
For their souls dwell in the house of tomorrow, which you cannot visit,
Not even in your dreams.
You may strive to be like them, but seek not to make them like you.
For life goes not backward nor tarries with yesterday.
You are the bows from which your children as living arrows are sent forth.
The archer sees the mark upon the path of the infinite,
And He bends you with His might that his arrows may go swift and far.
Let your bending in the archer's hand be for gladness;
For even as He loves the arrow that flies,
So He loves also the bow that is stable.

MY BOYS
Maggie Julo

After my husband, my two sons were the most important people in my life! All I ever dreamed of as a teenager was being married and having children. I wanted to give my children all the opportunities I felt that I never had.

My dream of children came true with two very different sons. Our older son, "Jackie," was serious and seemed to know at an early age just what he wanted from life. David, on the other hand, just wanted to have fun!

We had a great life together. As many families did, we took part in little league baseball, soccer, football, school programs, and plays. I was extremely close to both my boys, and there was absolutely nothing I would not do for them...unless it was against the law!

Jackie graduated from college with a degree in Aerospace Engineering and a Master's degree in Civil Engineering. We were so proud of him. He was the first to marry, and he and his wife gave birth to two beautiful grandchildren, Jack III and Jennifer.

David had a much different school experience and decided to quit school in his senior year of high school. He eventually obtained a GED and enrolled in Penn State Technical School. But after only one month in college, David became seriously ill and at age eighteen was diagnosed with Crohn's Disease. His life became a "living hell." The only bright spots were when he met and married his wife, Tricia, and welcomed their beautiful daughter, Destiny, into their lives. She really was "his life."

David lived in agony…through nine surgeries and constant pain. Through all the endless hospitalizations and horrific side effects, he always took comfort in his daughter, Destiny. She seemed to be the one who could always give him comfort and hope. The disease also took its toll on his marriage, and it ended in divorce. It was then that we took David back to our home to care for him. We felt that as long as he had Destiny by his side, he could retain some hope and dignity. His horrible life was made bearable by our time together with Destiny and with David.

Then, the unimaginable happened. He lost the use of both of his legs. The blood flow was unable to go through his bones to his feet… and his bones were becoming more and more brittle. He was then confined to a wheelchair and his bed. His bedroom then became his only existence. He would plead with us to take Destiny to Jackie's house for the weekend so she could play with her cousins in some type of normalcy. As the time passed, he became very depressed, and we believe he "gave up on life."

Through these horrible years the "four of us" (my husband Jack, son David, Destiny, and me) would travel to Indiana to visit Jackie and his family. Jackie's family would travel back to Pennsylvania to visit us, and our sons retained their extremely close relationship. My son, Jackie, always came to help me when David was hospitalized or when I just needed some help in caring for everyone. While he was traveling for his job, Jackie also checked in with me at least three times a week by phone. Many times he would tell me that he "just needed to stay awake," and I would worry about his welfare, too. However, these phone calls became a "lifeline" for me, and I was extremely grateful that my sons cared so much for me. I was very blessed.

David was hospitalized for the last time on October 15, 2007. He had another blockage and needed another surgery. The doctors completed all the tests and scheduled him for surgery the next morning. My fear was that he had "waited too long" for this surgery, but my mind again went into optimism…hoping that this would make him "well" again for at least another year.

After work that day, I immediately went to the hospital to visit David and found Jackie at his side. Our son, Jackie and his family, had moved back to Pennsylvania about two years before this fateful day. My husband and I went out to a nearby restaurant with Jackie for dinner. We were gone for only an hour, and my husband dropped us off at the hospital and said he would see David the next day after his surgery.

When Jackie and I entered the room, we found that David had vomited, and no one had come in to help him. We immediately washed him, changed his clothing, and tried to comfort him. Jackie stayed for another hour and then left for the one hour trip to his home. He promised to return the next day after the surgery. David told me that he was having a difficult time breathing. The nurse checked his oxygen level and told us it was "okay." I remained with my precious son until after midnight. He was still awake, and I asked him if it was alright for me to go home and get some sleep. I was driving a school bus at that time in my life and needed some rest before my morning run at 5:45 a.m. I kissed him goodnight as I had a thousand times before and said, "I love you, and I should be back by 8:30 a.m." He said "goodnight" and told me "I love you, too, mom."

Little did I know then that those words would be his last ones to me. Our phone rang at 2:30 a.m. telling us that David was in ICU and that we should come immediately. On the way, I called Jackie, and he said he would come "ASAP". I knew it would be at least an hour and a half before he could possibly be there.

When we arrived, the doctor told us that the nurses had found him "not breathing" and did not know how long he had been without oxygen. I screamed, "Please tell me he's not going to die!" There was no answer from the doctor. As I entered his room, I was shocked to see that David was now on life support with all types of IVs running between him and the machines. There were two nurses with him, and all I could do was sit beside him, hold his hand, and pray. I never stopped my prayers until Jackie arrived.

I called David's former wife, Tricia, and told her what was happening. I asked her to come to the hospital, and at 5:00 a.m., I called my boss to report our situation. By about 5:30 a.m., close family members who Jackie had called started to arrive. I could only hug them...I couldn't talk at all. Jackie called our priest, and he came to administer the "last rites" and stayed with us.

Later that morning, after many more tests, the doctors told us that there was no change in David...that he had "no brain waves." He had no blood pressure on his own. He told us there was "no hope" and asked us to make the dreaded decision to turn off the ventilator.

I jumped up from his bedside, turned to everyone, and cried: "I can't make this decision on my own. I brought him into this world, and I don't want to be the one who decides to 'take him out' of this world." They all expressed their opinions when the priest turned to me and said, "Maggie, he's already with the Lord. Pulling that plug is not going to make a difference."

So on October 16, 2008, at 12:36 p.m. my dear son's heart stopped beating for the last time.

Jackie spoke to the priest, and a funeral director was recommended. We were asked if we wanted an autopsy, and we declined. He had gone through enough. Everyone left the room. The nurses removed the IVs, and the doors were closed with the curtains drawn. There was a basin of soap and water, and for the very last time, I washed my dear son and said goodbye to my precious boy.

Most of the arrangements were made by Jackie as he tried to spare us this duty. One of the most dreadful times for us happened the next day when people came to remove his hospital bed and his wheelchair. My husband and son took the ramp apart in front of our home. This was truly the end of my life as I had known it for years.

That day, I washed the shirt that David wore that last day in the hospital and folded it neatly. I keep it on my bedroom dresser. I occasionally pick it up, hold it close, and as I "smell" the fabric, my memories come flooding back.

They say that "life goes on." I thought my nightmare was finally over when David died, but my life took on a new "turn" when I was diagnosed in April as having had a "silent heart attack." Atrial fibrillation was now my constant companion. During the month following David's death, our son, Jackie, set up a bereavement counseling appointment with Sylvia for the entire family. We started our journey to healing the deepest wound any parent can ever suffer. I felt that we were making some very slow progress trying to decide to "live again."

But then, just nineteen months after we lost our David, Jackie's wife called me early in the morning to tell us that our beloved son, Jackie, had died at 10:58 p.m. on May 27, 2009. His autopsy showed that the lower chambers of his heart stopped pumping, and he died instantly.

The shock of this news sent me into a place that is so black, so deep, it cannot be fathomed. I blamed myself both times. First, I blamed myself for not staying at the hospital all night with David, and I blamed myself for giving Jackie the "wrong genes." David was thirty-six years of age when he died, and Jackie was just forty-one. How could this happen to us?

I feel that I am truly in a nightmare from which we may never wake up. My three grandchildren have no fathers, and we no longer have "our boys." Our only salvation has been our faith in God, our grandchildren, and our grief counselor, Sylvia. I believe she truly "saved our lives." I will end with this truth: I pray that God will bless us all, and I believe that we will all be together once again in Heaven. As it states in the Bible, "We grieve, but not as those who have no hope."

Maggie Julo
November 2011

IN LOVING MEMORY OF MY FATHER
JACK BERNARD JULO, JR.
Jack Bernard Julo, III

The following "manuscript" was sent to me by Jack Julo, III, who lost his father in 2009. He was sixteen years of age. He wrote this immediately after he returned home after his dad's funeral. I have left the manuscript "as it was received" without any corrections for grammar or "flow." I believe that his words were flowing from his very proud, but broken heart! Sylvia Silvetti Havlish

My Father, (Jack Bernard Julo, Jr.) was the Senior Vice President of Sun Building Systems located in Taylor, Pennsylvania. But others like myself know him as a caring, loving, smart, athletic, intelligent, friendly, outgoing, fun-loving and a crazy dancer, etc. There just aren't enough words to describe my dad.

He was a genuinely fantastic, extraordinary dad, son, brother, uncle, cousin, grandson, husband, godfather, and of course, to many an exceptional good friend. (sigh) I wish he could have been a grandfather as well for he would have been the greatest. Including myself we all love him and miss him, we all want him to be here, but we all must accept that he is in a better place with other loved ones including David Matthew Julo, his brother and that place is the Kingdom of God aka Heaven. It's unfortunate, and unfair that Jack or "Jackie" had to leave us at such a young age of forty-one years, eleven months, and ten days old (1967-2009), but it is a natural part of life: we are all born and we all must die and be welcomed into the loving arms of Jesus Christ our Savior and our Father God. My dad did not suffer, he did not complain, he was just living his life to the fullest. He loved everybody in his life, and he is watching over all of us and smiling as he does it.

Even though my father Jack is not physically here, he still is emotionally and spiritually here, and he will always be in our hearts and in our memories, which we all will cherish and never forget. He had a tremendous amount of friends who he would do anything for, he loved all you guys, and I thank you for being such great and close friends to my father. He talked very highly about all of you guys often, with some wild and funny stories.

Special thanks to everyone who came to either the viewing and / or funeral for my father. We must all rejoice for my dad, who is now in heaven. He was proud of me, my sister Jenifer Lynn Julo, and his niece Destiny Ann Julo, and madly in love with his wife since 1984, Barbra Ann Julo (maiden name, Hunsberger). He loved, cared, and respected his parents Jack Bernard Julo Sr. and Margaret Ann Julo so much. And most importantly we must never forget the man Jack Bernard Julo, Jr. Thank you so much, dad, for all of the great memories and everything that you taught me and did for me. R.I.P. Dad, I love you so much, I miss you so much, I'll never forget you, and I'll pass on the Julo name in honor of you dad (Jack Bernard Julo IV).

Love, your son always,
Jack Bernard Julo III XOXOXO

Love Now and Always,
Your son, Jack Bernard Julo III

TO MY DAD...

I always have these tears to cry,
And I'm left with questions of why?
I have such strong feelings,
If only you could see.
But I have lost you.
What is loss?
Some may never know,
Others know too well.
For I love you like shadows love moonlight
And when I look to the sky at night,
I cry,
Because I know that's where you are.
Love and miss you Dad

Jenny (Ford) Julo, 2011

Note from author:

Jenny Julo is the daughter of Jack Julo, Jr. who died when Jenny was thirteen years old. Her poem was written when she was fifteen years of age, just two years after her dad passed away.

Leigh Fritz

THE LIGHT OF LEIGH
Diann Hammel

I was seventeen years old when I got married and had Leigh. She was a beautiful baby who came into the world with a little smile on her face. She was a very content baby. She changed my life, and I have no regrets having her when I was so young. I enjoyed her and loved her so much. She was my "Lil Sidekick!" We grew up together.

Once she started talking, she was a little "jabber jaw," always giggling and happy. She had these beautiful blue eyes and a sweet smile. At the age of four, she started dance lessons and continued throughout her school years right up to graduation. She was asked to teach some classes, and we traveled to Disney many times for her to dance there. She learned to play guitar from a pastor in a youth group, was a Girl Scout, and sang in the choir. She seemed wise beyond her years.

She loved to help people. Some have told me that if they needed to talk to someone, they would call Leigh. That also was my habit. Her brother, Eric, was born four years after she was, and since the time he arrived, she worried and mothered him, too. They became very close.

I remember getting together with her as an adult to do some shopping and go for a bite to eat. We also exercised together. We would always end up laughing so hard until the tears would run out. We had fun just acting silly. Many people thought we were sisters, not really mother/daughter. We thought alike, looked alike, and laughed alike. She would look at me and say, "Hey, don't laugh like I do!" Then we would only laugh more.

She would come over, and we would cook and bake together. She was blossoming into a fine young woman. She valued her family, and the time we spent together. If I had to think of some words to describe her spirit, it would be "loving, caring, and full of jubilation." She loved that word. That says so much about her.

She was also very talented in areas other than her singing, playing guitar, etc. She could knit, crochet, and loved to give hand-made gifts which I will always treasure now. She experienced the deaths of her Nana at thirteen years of age and her Grandmother at age seventeen. She was so close to both of them and really mourned their passing. I would always worry that if something happened to me, she would not have any female figure in her life. Little did I know then that in the last ten years I have lost my first mother-in-law, my mother, my grandmother, and now, my precious daughter. I feel lost and robbed. In fact, I feel like a book on a shelf without bookends.

Two weeks before Leigh's accident, she became a godmother. She was so excited and wanted to make her godchild some baby blocks like I had made for her while I was pregnant with Leigh. They were made of yarn on canvas. She so wanted to give them to her little goddaughter on her first birthday. When I would see her unfinished blocks after her death, I knew that I wanted to finish them for her… and I did. I gave them to her godchild on her first birthday. It brings back my last Mother's Day with Leigh. John and I were sitting on the patio, and she came around the corner as she always did…saying: "Hey!" She was bright-eyed and jubilant. She gave me her usual hug and kiss, her "Happy Mother's Day" greeting, and a beautiful mini "carnival" Petunia plant. She sat down and pulled out the block with the letter "Z" from her purse. As we were talking and admiring her work, John's chair broke, and he fell to the ground. After we knew he was okay, we broke out into more laughter.

Then, we walked her to the front yard, and she quickly sat in my new Jeep. She was laughing even more now, and in fact, I took a picture of her and John and the Jeep. We hugged and kissed again, and then John and I watched her leave. I remember thinking how lucky I was to have such a beautiful daughter inside and out. That was Sunday, May 8.

On Monday, May 9, after work I walked into my dining room, and this thought just jumped into my head. I even said to myself, "My God, why would you even be thinking about that?" My fourth grade teacher lost her twenty-six year old daughter in a car accident. It was her only child. I was told she was never the same after that. I remember telling myself, "That's awful...why am I thinking about that? Where did it even come from?"

Thursday, May 12. I made some plans with Leigh to go to her house and get some rocks for my garden. I called her because I had one of my bad headaches. I told her I didn't know if I could lift them that day, but I'd still come over. I lie down on her couch. Then she was showing me some shoes on her laptop computer. I got up and sat next to her—and then once again, burst into laughter. Why? As I sat down, we "mushed" into each other. We continued our girl talk about shoes, that she was going to teach me to crochet, and I would teach her to paint. I asked her if she had ever painted a picture, and she ran upstairs and came back with a picture she had painted. It was a painting of gates in the clouds...very dark, but peaceful. She said she had painted it a while ago.

My head hurt, and I wanted to get to bed early. I gave her a hug and a big, wet kiss, and we went outside. I was standing in the street by my Jeep, and she was on the sidewalk. She was walking back and forth and waving her hands up and down like "jumping jacks." She called to me that she and her friends had decided to start doing "old lady things." When I laughed and asked her what that meant, she said they were going to start a card night on the third or fourth Monday of every month and take turns at each other's homes. She was really looking forward to that. We said our "I love you" again, and I drove away, never knowing that it would be the very last time

I saw my daughter alive.

Friday, May 13. My husband and I work two separate shifts, so I take him his supper and sit with him some times. I usually leave about 6:30 or so. As I was heating his supper, my cell phone rang at 6:27 pm. I didn't recognize the number so I didn't answer. Only my children and my husband have my cell phone number. Then my house phone rang. I briefly thought that "something was up" because of the house phone ringing immediately after the cell phone. I said "Hello. Hello."

Then I heard my ex-father-in-law say, "Diann, this is Pa. It's Leigh.",

"What about Leigh?" I asked. He didn't answer. I repeated, "Pa, what about Leigh?"

"She was in a car accident."

I spoke calmly, "Is she okay?"

"I don't think so. I think she's gone."

"Where did you get this information?"

He explained that she was following Jess to her house and a truck hit her. Jess's mom drove to Leigh's grandfather's house to tell him. The accident happened at 5:45 p.m. and I got word by 6:30. I told him that I had to get off the phone...and that I would call him back.

I hung up and dropped to the floor and yelled, "No! No!, Not my Leigh. Please don't take my Leigh." My son had been home and had just left before I got the phone call. I called him as I cried, "Eric, come home right now!"

He was home so fast. He came in. I said that I thought Leigh was killed in a car accident. He grabbed me and hugged me so tight I had bruises under my arms. I had to ask him to let go as he was hurting me. Then, I called my husband, John at work. I was hysterical. When he asked me what was wrong, I repeated again that I thought Leigh was killed in a car accident. He said he'd be right home, and like Eric, he arrived very quickly. I kept saying "I think" she's been killed because we hadn't heard anything "officially" yet.

Talk about minutes turning into hours...this was it. Eric called

Leigh's cell phone, but there was no answer. John called the State Police, but they gave us no information. I didn't know Jess's phone number, but Eric got it and called her. All she could do was cry. From 6:30 until 8:30, we could get no definite information.

I called my Dad and asked him to come over. When he arrived, my husband stepped outside and told him that Leigh was in a car accident. He asked if she was gone. "Yes," John answered. My dad's eyes filled with tears, and he shook his head in disbelief. Leigh was his oldest grandchild.

Family and friends started arriving, and then around 8:45 p.m. a State trooper's car and the coroner pulled up to our home. Then the reality started to hit home. I went through crying when I first heard the news and then not being able to cry because of the disbelief that this could actually have taken place. I remember the coroner kneeling down in front of me and placing Leigh's purse on my lap. It felt as if the whole evening was an "out of body" experience. How could my daughter be gone?

It was then that I was told the details. Leigh was following her friend, Jessica. A man in a pickup truck, coming the opposite direction, was speeding and swerving. Jess got out of the way, but Leigh had no place to go. She could only pull a little way over because of a guardrail. The truck hit Leigh's car "head on" killing her instantly.

The crash was horrific. Leigh was a very safe driver, and she "babied" her car. She was proud of her car and had bought it "almost new" by herself. The truck hit her so hard the front of her car was gone, and the engine was thrown into the street. The truck was bent in half. The front wheels were touching the back like an upside down letter "V." The worst part about this was that the driver of the truck was very, very drunk.

This accident did not have to happen. My daughter should be here. We should not have to die because of someone else's negligence. Leigh was against drinking and driving. Unfortunately her friend, Jess, has to have these images forever in her head. I'm human, and I have to admit this: I find justice in the fact that the man was thrown out of his vehicle and killed also. It is hard enough losing my daughter and then having to deal with the possibility of him living and getting away with this. I think it would have driven me crazy. However, as time has passed, John and I saw a picture of him. A reaction took place we were not expecting. Both of us "choked up" and got very teary-eyed knowing that this man's life is over—and there is a family out there hurting like we are hurting.

There are so many emotions to deal with…every day a different one. Some days there are five in one day. I am sad, depressed, mad, angry, empty, crying and bitter.

I remember asking the coroner if I would be permitted to see my daughter. Thankfully, he said yes. When we saw her, she was flawless. She had suffered all internal injuries. About midnight, the house was empty except for my son, my husband, and me. We were trying to take this all in…to make some sense. I remember thinking that "… my daughter won't be home tonight in her bed. She won't ever get married, have a baby…all things she looked so forward to doing."

I had things to pass down to her. Now what? Not only is my daughter gone, but my best friend, too. Children shouldn't die before their parents. This isn't the proper order. Just then the funeral director called to tell me that they now had her body. We made arrangements for the next morning.

When we arrived the next day, we immediately asked to see her. I remember this so clearly. I walked in first. Eric hesitated, and John grabbed his hand to guide him in. "Let's go see your sister."

We all cried…cried hard. I just needed to touch her, hold her, tell her I was sorry for what happened to her. We wanted so much more for her. We sat awhile and then went in the next room to make the arrangements.

Over the next several days, we had to make more trips to the funeral home. Each time we would go into the room to see her. We probably visited a half dozen times, and I think this was so helpful in the way that we were not totally shocked the day of the service.

We had time to adjust the best that we could. On one of the visits, I remember pulling up a chair, holding her hand, and stroking her face. I had about a thirty minute one-sided conversation with her. It was very hard. But as I reflect back on this time, it was a time to touch and say goodbye. I could tell her how much I loved her and how blessed and lucky we were to have had such a beautiful daughter.

I exchanged my hair with hers. They cut some hair from underneath her head and gave it to me. I had my husband cut some of my hair, and we tied a purple bow around it and weaved it through her fingers. We also wrote notes to her and placed them against her heart. We also made two big picture boards with photos from the beginning of life until the end.

It was honestly the most beautiful funeral I had ever attended. There were so many flowers that filled the room and made it almost cheery. This was a time to take it all in. As difficult as it was, we wanted to remember this. We wanted to make her last visit with us as special as we could. As the days passed and her funeral came, I was again amazed at how many lives this young lady of twenty-six years had touched. Hundreds of people came to say goodbye to Leigh... each with something special to say and remember.

My oldest brother said it best. "A lot of love passed through that funeral home. You can be a fountain or a drain in life. Leigh was definitely a fountain." My son and I both spoke at the service as did her friends.

I remember staying at the grave site until the end. Instead of being the first one to put the flower on her casket, we were the last ones. We watched Eric as he waited for his sister to be lowered into the ground. He was on his hands and knees, making sure the lid stayed on and was secure.

About five or six weeks out, a big wave of reality hits, and you really start to miss her in a way you can't imagine. We yearned to touch her, talk with her, and feel her near us. Eric said he really misses her and is grieving for his future. He always assumed he would have his older sister to help him with aging parents. My husband, John, loved her like his very own daughter. I thank God for Eric, John, my family, and Sylvia.

My husband loves me so much, and I couldn't get through this without him. He wrote the following poem for me and for Leigh.

WITHOUT LIMITS

by

John Hammel

You are no longer in our realm
and your absence here
fills our eyes with tears.
And without you in this place
means we can't share a smile
or sit down and talk awhile.
The bar has been lowered since you've been gone
and for so many will not be replaced
by your wit, charm and simple grace.
But in the knowledge of
the new place you call home
there is only comfort; you're far from alone.
An angel in heaven
you now know all the secrets of life and beyond.
You've been given a magic wand.
One day soon our time will also come.
We're eager to see you again
so you can introduce us to where you've been.
There will be so much to show us
and to have been so sad we were dim wits
Because you beat us to this place without limits!
For two beautiful souls…Leigh & Diann

To summarize my feelings, I remember how it has gone from the first call when I fell to the floor and shouted out. Then, I went numb with disbelief. There was lots of crying and no appetite. I was very exhausted and felt like I was in a "daze." I was very empty. I experienced deep pain everywhere...in my stomach, my head. Then you question yourself...you ask all the "whys." I briefly lost my faith...I could not understand why God would do this to her... to me...to our family and friends. I was so depressed it was hard to get up in the morning or to finish any tasks. In the grocery store, I would be overcome with anxiety, leave my cart, and run out. I would go home and just wanted to keep my head down and not be seen. I knew at this point that I needed help. I went to a local support group and that's how I met Sylvia. What a good decision that was for me. It was good to be able to listen to other people in similar circumstances. We could cry together and talk about overcoming the different feelings we all go through. Sylvia was wonderful...listening, validating, and sharing her own experience. She was there when I needed her. It took me about six months just to start to feel like doing anything again. It's still limited.

I still visit Leigh's grave and lay down on a tarp and just cry. I do get some peaceful days now, but then the feelings build up again. I just cry and let them out. We talk. We miss her so much, and sometimes it is still difficult to believe that this has really happened. However, I take special comfort in remembering something that one of the women who worked with Leigh shared with me. It really sums up her life.

At work, Leigh told her this: "If I can touch one life a day and make someone happy, then I am happy."

Be happy, my sweet Leigh...the light of my life!

Losing David...Finding Jacquelyn
Sylvia Silvetti Havlish

When the sound of the ringing phone startled me from my work that December day in 2002, I never imagined that it would be my beloved nephew, David. Just two years before this, he had simply "disappeared" from our family radar. He grew up in San Antonio, Texas, and the distance between there and Pennsylvania meant that our together times were too short and too far in between.

But his voice was bright, cheery, and so calm. I should have known, I thought later. I am a counselor. How could I not have known?

As we caught up on his life and his future plans to come north from Florida, his new state of residence, my heart was filled with love and anticipation. We were going to celebrate my mom's, David's grandmother's, ninetieth birthday. I begged him to come up sooner than later and be here to surprise her on January 5th. He said he would "try" to change his plans to be here on that date, and then he proudly announced that he found out that he "had a daughter, Jacquelyn." All David ever wanted in his life was a loving family. He was thirty-seven years old and had been searching for this all his life.

The pride and love in his voice for this now fourteen-year-old daughter was filling the airways. He told me about his plans to take her red roses on her fourteenth birthday on Dec. 30th. I said I knew she would love them. I also said I couldn't wait until our family could meet our "new" great-granddaughter, niece, and daughter! He was strangely silent then. But that silence would later be explained.

As I came in from an errand just one day before my mother's surprise birthday party, my son greeted me at the door with tears streaming down his face. He was whispering so that my mother would not hear. He was shaking with grief. The Florida police had called to tell us that our beautiful David was dead. Unthinkably, he had taken his own life on New Year's Eve. Then the realization that every family of suicide finally figures out hit me like a rock.

His calm, serene voice the night of his phone call now told me the story. He had "made up his mind"...resolved his issues...made his decision. He knew the end was near, and he was saying goodbye to all of us. If only I had figured that out. If only.

The shock of telling my mother the horrible news took over for the next few hours and then the further shock of trying to make the "final arrangements" with the Florida police. His mother and father had both died, and his only brother was in Alaska. And so I was suddenly thrown into the "club" no one ever wants to be in...family victims of suicide.

In my heart I kept hearing him telling me that he "had a daughter...Jacquelyn." But of course I knew not where or how to find her. I had no idea what her last name might be or how to begin.

And then eight years later, she found me! She told me she had been trying to track down David's family for many years. The police finally gave her my name and phone number. Although we had moved, I have the same phone number, and there she was on the other end of the line.

Her sweet voice hesitated as she told me her name. As soon as I heard "Jacquelyn," I somehow knew. This was Jacquelyn! This is my niece. I remember almost screaming into the phone that I was so thankful to hear her voice. She was relieved. I was ecstatic.

Our relationship is just beginning long distance. But I am thanking God for bringing David's beautiful daughter into our lives. I will embrace her. For after all, it is my way of embracing my sweet David.

Rest in peace, my beautiful boy...I have welcomed your precious daughter into my heart.

Sylvia Silvetti Havlish   November 2011

"Don't Look Back…You'll Fall Over What Is In Front Of You"
Pat Youkanis-Warmkessel

My beautiful baby, Nicholas, was born on January 17, 1969. He was a healthy, nine-pound little bundle of joy. My life seemed complete. But when he was just three years old, he suffered a petite mall seizure which kept escalating until he was having grand mall seizures. The doctors put him on high doses of anti-seizure medications but to no avail.

We were then referred to Children's Hospital in Philadelphia where the doctors performed many tests with no confirmed diagnosis. It was decided that they would do surgery and remove a small section from the frontal part of his brain. It was then that we had a diagnosis of a genetic brain disorder known as Baton Mayo syndrome. There was no cure, and we were told to prepare for the death of our little boy.

He lived until March 23, 1974 when he passed away in our home. The priest who was officiating at Nick's funeral took me aside and asked me to describe what I was feeling. I voiced the feeling that any parent would say: "Why Nick? Why not someone else?"

"Who?" he asked. "Could you choose someone here to take his place?"

Of course, I could not. And then he said something I have never forgotten: "Stop looking back; you may fall over something that is right in front of you." That has been very good advice throughout the course of my life. I always pass this on to grieving people, and they seem to understand what I'm saying.

My husband and I went to genetic counseling, and they found that there would be a twenty-five percent chance that our next child would have the same disease. It was then we decided not to have any more children. We felt that we could not knowingly do this to another precious child and that we both could not go through another loss like this.

In June of the same year that Nick died, I decided to go back to work. Staying at home day after day was too difficult for me so I decided to find a job. I was hired as a part-time secretary for the Magisterial District Judge in my township. I enjoyed my job and worked my way up to full-time office manager, office supervisor for all the fourteen court secretaries. After twenty years in that office, the judge I was working for retired. I decided to campaign for the position and won in 1995. I served as a district judge for fourteen years and retired in 2008. I now serve as a senior judge and fill in when a judge is on long-term sick leave.

My strong belief in God and the help of my family helped me to get through the years of grief and regret. As the priest said, "Don't look back; you will fall over what is in front of you!"

I will always miss and love my sweet son, but I know that when God calls me home, I will be with Nicholas again.

Always loving him...Mom

Pat E. Youkanis-Warmkessel

I NAMED MY BABY BLUE
Elizabeth Marcon

Grief is not a linear path. Some days I reel back further than I thought I ever was. Tomorrow is not always better. But I am starting to think about "the early days" as being different from where I am now.

My baby died when I was twenty-five weeks and three days pregnant. He was stillborn on August 10, 2011. I never held him. I held him with my eyes in one disorienting moment, his crumpled face and tiny hands forever etched into my soul, unable to reconcile what I saw with what I thought I would see. He was beautiful and perfect. Eventually I named him Blue. It seemed like a nickname at first, but soon it became so perfectly his name. I knew he was real when other people called him Blue.

My grief was, in a word, unspeakable. Looking back I don't know how I functioned, and looking back, I'm not sure that I did. I found incredible solace in thoughts of going to sleep and never waking up. At the same time I didn't want to go to sleep, because I didn't want to wake up. I was told it would get better. I was told time would heal.

I counted every day to his due date. "I should be thirty-eight weeks pregnant today. My baby should still be with me, in my arms if not in my belly." When almost three months had passed, I was still thinking about him every day. I was still missing him and loving him every day. And I was still feeling like nothing could take the hurt away.

~

These are not the early days. It's been over six months now. Others have forgotten. But for me the hurt is still not gone. I try to find joy in one little thing each day. When I can find one little thing to smile about, I make a tiny move forward. Though joy is not what it used to be. It's all relative. So I redefine the word. Joy is desire, joy is "not sad," joy is distraction. When I have joy, the new—perhaps distorted—kind, I take it.

Though other times I want to smash things. I want to break a glass on tile floor, break it into a million tiny pieces. I don't even care if then I have to sweep it up. There is something soothing and symbolic in the act of putting it all away afterwards.

~

The holidays had to come amidst my mourning. I had imagined cradling my newborn son on Thanksgiving. I had imagined my baby's first Christmas, surrounded by cooing relatives. Instead I spent Christmas morning alone. I stayed with my sick grandmother while her caregiver went to church. I looked around at her decorations and photos and holiday cards...there were my niece and nephew, there was my one-year-old nephew...and there was a missing card of a missing newborn great-grandson. When I returned to my parent's house in tears, they asked what happened. Nothing. Nothing happened. I went out into their yard and sat in front of the tree we planted on Blue's due date. I whispered to the branches, I closed my eyes and breathed deeply, sending energy from my heart, through Blue's tree, to the core of the earth, through Blue's tree, up and out into the universe, back through Blue's tree and back to my heart.

"You're always with me, buddy."

I looked up at his big blue sky. I leaned over to kiss the skinny trunk of his tree. I stood up in damp and dirty yoga pants, went inside to change into something suitable for guests and for Christmas. I drank two glasses of Champagne before I ate anything for the day.

From then on, it was easier to pretend there was nothing wrong.

But these are not the early days. And sometimes I have to pretend there's nothing wrong. Because other people forget. And other people get pregnant, and other people have babies, and sometimes I know these people and I have to pretend I am not angry inside. Angry at how life just...goes on.

It's been over six months now. I am still on anti-depressants. Each night is now filled with sleep, but also filled with all-too-life-like dreams, and I can't always distinguish real life from the dreams. They are crazy and vivid even though almost exclusively still in black and white.

~

I'm not sure when I stopped wanting to die. Somewhere in the way that life just went on, it started moving on for me too. The heavy fog of my sadness began to burn off slowly, without my really knowing it. I don't mind thinking that the sun had come out. Still some days my grief is anything but pure. Some days it is so much anger and frustration it is rage. Some days I am still irritable. Some days I am belligerent. Some days, still, I am brittle, unpredictable, and utterly inconsolable.

But these are not the early days, and many days I feel light. The dark days are shorter, are less dark, and are fewer and further between. I may still not like where I am, but I am getting somewhere.

And everywhere I go, I know I'm not alone. My baby travels with me. His name is Blue. With a capital "B." My baby's name is Blue.

Harvey McGarry, Jr.

A Son's Legacy

Laura McGarry

December 27, 2011

To the Weekend Girlfriend:

Remember Harv? The guy you spent that boozy Saturday with ten months ago? That Saturday. That final day. I don't know you. Indeed, I never heard your name spoken, not even your existence mentioned, until that final Saturday morning before Harv left our house. But since you were the last person to see Harv alive... and likely the first person to know he was dead...there are some things about Harv that I need to tell you about now.

Today is Harv's birthday...two months, almost exactly to the day, from when he died in his sleep sometime late at night in that motel room nearly a year ago. Funny, today is a Tuesday, and Harv was born on a Tuesday. Tonight, though, it was a very different kind of Tuesday for us. We lit candles, all right, but not in celebration. We lit five candles for Harv in commemoration...one for each of us who love him dearly and miss him so much... his Dad and me, his sister Tammy, brother-in-law Steven, and his ten-year-old nephew Alex. And as we lit the candles, we each read a passage from a poem in his memory and quietly cried together.

This picture is one of the last photos taken of Harv just a few months before he died. Nice shot, isn't it? You can see his smile and humor as he gently waves away the surprise photographer. It was Thanksgiving weekend of 2010 at a family gathering in Ohio. Earlier that day, the newest baby in the family was baptized, and Harv was named as Logan's godfather. He was proud of that. Maybe he even mentioned Logan to you that final Saturday as you leaned across a table and drank together? Maybe he also told you about Logan's father and mother, Rich and Mary, Harv's cousins and best friends in life? This has been a hard year for Rich and Mary and their children as they grieve this absence, this hole in their lives. It's been a hard year for all of his other cousins, aunts, uncles and lifetime friends, too. A hard year borne, a big hole left for all of us.

That's because Harv was the kind of guy who had a real presence in our lives. He didn't simply show up at Thanksgiving dinner every five years. Those family gatherings in Ohio and Pennsylvania and other states...there were loads of them over the years, and he was there for most, no matter how far away he lived at the time. The holidays and reunions, the birthdays and graduations, the wedding and the funerals...he thought nothing of flying across the country for an anniversary celebration or driving 400 miles for a child's special birthday party or an aunt's confirmation or an uncle's hospitalization.

There were weekends at home in Pennsylvania, clay shooting with his Dad, golfing with his Ohio cousins, or deep-sea fishing with his Florida cousins. Anywhere folks and friends could meet for Super Bowls or for X-Men movies or just for snacks and beers were commonplace for my son. He was our family organizer, the one who took care of the hotel reservations and flight arrangements and the tee times for our "no-guts-no-glory reunion" golf tournaments. He was the one we could always count on to pick up folks at the airport, to run for forgotten groceries, to drive the grandmothers, or to serve as pallbearer. He kept all our ducks in a row, kept us on time and on schedule, and kept us laughing and talking along the way. Things were always more fun and interesting when Harv was there, and yes, family time meant just about everything to him. "Family and football," we used to joke, but we always knew what was really first.

Life's disappointments started catching up with Harv that last year before his death. It was a tough year for him. For one thing, he went too long without a job, something both astonishing and discouraging for him at the same time. He wasn't where he wanted to be, where he thought he would be at this stage of life. He took medications and was drinking too much…a dangerous mix for sure. And during this time of vulnerability, many of us tried to throw him a "life saver." It would seem, though, on that final day, that you and your pals threw him a concrete block instead. Maybe you could have helped him more that day? Maybe not. Who knows now. I guess there is no point in wondering. The choices are long gone, and nothing now can change the way things turned out.

But I wish you knew the Harv that we did. You had that one last day with him, but for us, there were thousands of days before that. A whole childhood of memories…teenage years and college experiences and shared fun times as adults. These were the kind of times that parents earn for years and treasure forever. Somehow I think you need to know that Harv's Dad still sobs every day. And me? Well, I pretty much just walk around half numb except for those shocking jolts of realization that he's not coming back. So, remember Harv. Don't let that single day define who he was. Remember him as we do…someone who was always there for us, a guy who was very smart and very funny, who was loving and caring, full of laughter and daredevil adventure, and with a heart as big as the lifetime of memories he leaves behind.

Signed,
Harv's Mom
Laura McGarry

WE LOSE OUR SIBLINGS

Our sisters and brothers can be the longest lasting relationship in life...if we are lucky! As we all think about our own memories of our time with our siblings, many emotions are elicited. I had two brothers. Dean was my mother's son from her first marriage, and he was seventeen years my senior. When I was born, he had enlisted in the Army and was gone. When he would return home for a "visit" three or more years would have passed, and I would only really know him personally in our adult years. Although many miles always separated us, I loved him and respected him from afar. When he died in the year 2000, I was devastated. Where had all our "tomorrows" gone?

My "little brother," Mike, was born when I was two. As he writes in his song, How Lucky We Were, our greatest toy was our imagination. We didn't have a television until I was about eight or nine years of age and that was probably the luckiest break we had! We are now closer than ever before and share so many incredible memories. The older we become, the more we like to remember and laugh. I am so glad that we still have each other.

But when my brother, Dean, passed away, the grieving I experienced was one of the loneliest and difficult paths I've had to walk. Why? My support system of friends and extended family members forgot so quickly. They had no "point of reference" in regard to Dean. Most of my friends had never met him (he lived in Texas for most of my adult life...I lived in Pennsylvania) and there was no "local" service for him. One of the most insensitive and disappointing exchanges I had was with one of my cousins on my dad's side of the family. When she called right after I had the news of his death, her response to me was, "But you didn't really know him that much, did you?" I was so hurt and shocked at her question, I think I just hung up on her!

It seems from the literature that it is one of the most difficult grief periods to experience for the remaining siblings. Thankfully there are some new resources that can be found online to help the remaining brothers and sisters. I thank the grieving "adult children" who have shared with us the stories of their path of grief.

MEMORIES OF LORI
Sherry Goerner

There was no one like my sister, Lori. She was the "best." I loved her and I miss her so very much.

In order to really understand our journey, we have to go back to the true beginning. Annette and Fayne Fritz welcomed three children into this world...Sherry, Lori and Allen. We lived in a great neighborhood filled with our playmates. Because we lived on a "dead-end" street, we had a bright street light...and one solid rule. When the street light went on, it was time to come in the house for the evening. It wasn't long until one night, Lori and I "tested the waters" of that rule. We stayed out after the street light came on and kept right on playing. When the other children finally went home, we ran to the front door...only to find it locked! We knocked, screamed, pleaded...but to no avail. Finally, our father came to the door and asked us if that light had "just come on." We were "busted!" We were required to sit outside on the porch until the lesson was firmly planted in our minds. It worked. After that night, when that light came on, we ran to the front door. Even when we reached adulthood, it remained a memory that we joked about for years.

Lori was always a "happy-go-lucky" child who spread love and joy wherever she went. We loved playing with our "Barbie" dolls and riding our bicycles together on that same "dead-end" street. When our baby brother, Allen, was born, he became the "live doll" in our world of fantasy. We put him in the stroller and pushed him in circles around that street. What fun we had.

We shared a room upstairs and a double bed. I remember getting so angry sometimes as my side of the room was neat and her side was messy! But, despite those differences, we always fell asleep holding hands, especially if we were scared. I remember that one night Lori started sleep walking and walked right into the closet door and frightened me. She proceeded down the steps and into my Mom's side of the bed. Of course I followed her because I didn't know where she was going. When Mom awakened, there we were: Lori sound asleep...and me trying to figure it out! My mom told me not to wake her...she told her to go back to bed...and she did! So did I. I couldn't wait until morning to tell her about her adventure. She never remembered any of it, and it became another great "sister story".

One of the highlights of our weekly experiences was visiting both sets of grandparents on Sunday. Our mother's parents lived on a small farm, and we delighted in hiking, picking flowers, and in the winter, riding our sleds. We would all eat together, watch the news, and then go on to our dad's parents. There we had cousins, and we'd all watch Lawrence Welk and Animal Kingdom. We would have a snack together, and then we would head for home. I believe that this helped to make our family bond even stronger.

Because I was the older sister, there were many times when Lori would want to "tag along" with me and my friends— and I would be furious. However, our parents insisted that I should allow Lori to be a part of these activities. At that time we had separate rooms about six feet apart from each other. One night we thought we heard someone break into our house, and we joined each other in the hall with a pair of my biggest, clunky shoes in hand. As we were sneaking down the stairs ready to fire off a shot of shoe, the streetlight lit up the room—and there was mom! We were relieved and started laughing thinking about the seconds that separated our mom from our shoes! It was another story we would talk about for years.

As the years went by, Lori graduated with a license in Cosmetology.

When she was taking her state boards, she needed me to be her "model" so she could demonstrate her ability to cut hair, style it, and apply makeup…on half my face. We had to drive to Harrisburg from our hometown for this test and there I was at the finish: teased up puffy hair and makeup on half my face. That's when our Dad announced that he felt like stopping at the mall! We made a mad dash to the ladies' room so that Lori could "fix me up!" We laughed about that once again for years!

She eventually got her license to be a teacher of cosmetology and worked in that field for many years. Everyone with whom she worked couldn't help but love Lori. She was happily married to her high school sweetheart, and they enjoyed their families and their dogs. She eventually joined Mary Kay Cosmetics and was extremely successful with her incredible "people skills" and that beautiful smile. It was during her time with Mary Kay that a dream was born inside her to become a public school teacher. It seemed like an overwhelming plan, but she did it! She gathered up her confidence and was accepted into a Bachelor's program at a local college. She worked her way through by continuing to build her Mary Kay business, work as a teacher's assistant with a city school system, and still managed to graduate with honors. She was incredible! It was during this time of her life that she started to have bouts of "not feeling well." The doctors told her it was probably "irritable bowel syndrome."

She was hired for her very first professional position as a high school English teacher and was ecstatic. She really loved "kids" and was so excited about her new job. She would have ninth and eleventh grade English classes. She had such wonderful ideas and big plans. She wanted to be the type of teacher who inspired children to strive to do their best and dream big!

Then, that horrible day arrived. She wasn't feeling well again and started to vomit blood. Kevin, her husband, rushed her to the emergency room and called us to join him there.

We were not prepared for what they had to tell us. She had Stage Four cancer of the bowel, and they felt there was not much left for them to do. That's when Lori's character and spirit really kicked in. She was determined to do whatever they could do to help her... because she was going to teach. You see, this disaster occurred on a Friday...and the following Monday was the first day of school. She had worked too hard to just give up before it ever started. She said that she didn't believe the Lord would let her get this close to her dream and then take it away. She said that it was not in His nature to be cruel. Right then and there she called her new school, Daniel Boone School District, and told them the situation. They told her get better and would keep her job open for her. "Isn't that just like God?" she said.

She asked me to go with her to all her doctor appointments, and I was happy to do that. As they spoke, I was writing it all down so we could remember later. We went for a second opinion in Philadelphia and then the chemo began. When she was weak and "wiped out" after her treatments, I would find out for her anything she needed to know. She called me her "bulldog!" I just wanted my sister to be well again, and I wanted everything to go "back to normal." It never did go back to that.

By the first week of January, she had responded well to the treatments and was finally permitted to start teaching school. She explained to her students what she was going through and why she had the infusion bag on her. She explained that they couldn't "catch it" from her, but that she would really welcome their help. Most of them complied beautifully and immediately "fell in love" with Lori. The parents of her students also expressed their love for this brave young woman and the wonderful lessons about life that she was teaching their children. Although there were some students who were determined to "give her a hard time" even in this situation, she took it in stride and never let on to them how much it hurt her. She was a champion.

She was able to finish out that year and begin the next one. She eventually had to have a power wheelchair so she could maneuver through the high school hallways and get to her desk. When she had some bad days, my parents, my husband, and my daughter would go over and help her correct papers and tests. We all tried to chip in and help her whenever we could.

She kept up her chemo treatments, had sores in her mouth much of the time, ended up in the hospital several times. However, she always believed she would beat this thing. She made us all believe it.

We had our parents' fiftieth wedding anniversary coming up and were planning a surprise for them. While she and I were at one of her doctor appointments, I asked the nurse if I could speak to her privately. When I asked if she thought Lori could make it until May, she assured me that she thought she could probably do that, but that after that, she wasn't certain about the length of time remaining. Lori was very, very sick.

Well, Lori kept her upbeat ways and always made us believe she was fine. Her conversations were always about concerns for others. We had many scares, but she would always pull through somehow. I was so happy that she and I lived only about ten minutes apart so that I could get there whenever she or Kevin would call me. Sometimes she just needed to get things off her chest and she wanted me. I was encouraging her, sharing her fears and tears, or just smoothing some wonderful lotion on her skin. All these "sister" things helped her to feel better and to smell nice! These were precious moments for us.

We got together for our mom's birthday at my brother's home. She was tired when they arrived and explained about her day. She had a parent conference before she left school, and they told her how glad they were that she was their son's teacher. That was a Friday. I told Lori to rest and that I wouldn't call her the next day, Saturday, so she could get some rest. I told her I loved her...as we always ended every conversation with our love for each other.

Little did I know at the time that this would be our last conversation. On Sunday when we came home from church, the answering machine was blinking with a message that we should get to the hospital as soon as possible...not one message, but two. My husband, Bob, tried to console me and convince me that things would be okay. But this time, I had a horrible feeling in my stomach and in my heart. I knew it was not good...not this time.

When I entered her hospital room, I was not prepared to see Lori that way. I went to her side, held her hand, noticed she was cold, and put her hand under the cover. The people there said that the hospital had a special light to keep her warm. Soon, Lori moved as if she was annoyed with me and pulled her hand out from under the cover. I could imagine that if she could have talked, I would have received a "what are you thinking" statement from her.

As we were all waiting, the room was filling up with people. Some came in for a short time and then left to make room for others. I did not leave her for a second. Then the room emptied out except for Kevin's two sisters, Allen and me. Soon, it was just Allen, Lori, and me... just the three of us again together for one last time. It was then that she left the earth.

At both of her viewings (one so the students could pay their respects and one before her burial next to our grandparents), we never expected the many, many people who waited in line to say goodbye to our sweet Lori. We heard from so many people about how she had touched their lives. The guidance counselors told us that the students she touched the most were the "difficult" problem children! It was really amazing to see all the people who loved Lori and came to say their final good-byes.

There was no one like my sister, Lori. She was the "best." I loved her and miss her so very much.

REMEMBRANCES OF MY BROTHER, JIM ROTH

Thomas Roth

My brother, Jim, was born on July 1, 1950, at high noon... in the middle of the day, in the middle of the year, and in the middle of the century. My mother always believed that was an omen of some kind.

Jim was a boy of summer, his favorite time of year. He had a flaming red flat top, bright blue eyes, freckles, and a smile that could kill. He looked like no one else in our family.

The summers seemed endless then, in those wonderful and simpler days of Allentown. Summers for Jim meant baseball games at the Patriots Park, family picnics in Lehigh Parkway, church clambakes at Dorney Park, deep sea fishing for porgies and blue fish at the Jersey shore, overnight camping in the woods near our home, strawberry shortcake dinners, trips with our father to softball tournaments, and after- the- games visits to a never-ending succession of neighborhood beer joints populated by heavyset German men. Jim sat at the bar eating "Slim Jims" and hardboiled eggs pickled in jars of pink liquid and playing shuffleboard games until he fell asleep. Most of the bartenders in Allentown knew Jim by name, although he was still in grade school!

Jim wore "Hop-a-long Cassidy" boots, a Roy Rogers' six gun and fought wild Indians...mostly Apaches and Comanches. He was GI Joe fighting "Japs" and "Krauts" although at the time Jim was unaware that everyone in the neighborhood, including his own family, were

"Krauts!" He liked Howdy Doody but was secretly afraid of Clara Bell the Clown. He yearned to join the Mickey Mouse Club, become a Mouseketeer, and hang out with Annette Funicello, on whom he had an early crush.

But mostly in his youth, Jim was Mickey Mantle…except for one brief period in the Summer of 1961 when he became Roger Maris. Jim was a natural on the ball field, quicksilver fast and shagged fly balls with grace and agility. He had an arm like a rifle, throwing runners out on the base path straight and true. His grandfather hit him ground balls long into the night, until the field was illuminated only by moonlight. My father, a gifted softball player himself, swelled with pride every time Jim stepped onto the field.

Jim was the "Natural" before Robert Redford played the role. Later in life, Jim became as handsome as Robert Redford. The girls loved him, which was at times a blessing and at times a curse for him.

As a kid, Jim ran everywhere. He was a human blur, in a constant state of rapid movement, not because he was in a hurry to get anywhere, and not even because he had any place to go, but because he just liked to run. He liked to run before running was considered a healthy thing to do, and even before it became fashionable. Jim ran the trails in Lehigh Parkway when it was only him, the squirrels, and a few dogs. It did not surprise me years later when he would run marathons, or when his son, Ryan, would become a cross country star at Dieruff High School. It was simply in the blood. When I think of Jim in years to come, he will be jogging on the trails in Lehigh Parkway near the stream where his ashes have settled.

Jim was a Phillies fan, except in October during the World Series when he conveniently switched to the Yankees. His favorite player was Richie Ashburn, who, like Jim, had red hair, an easy smile and shagged flies effortlessly in center field. Jim tried to bat left-handed for a time to emulate his idol. Jim later switched his allegiance to Mike Schmidt, who at least batted right-handed.

Jim loved the Allentown Fair because in those days we got off from school to go to the Fair. He always loved the smells of the Fair, the food, even the smells of the farm animals. He was fascinated by the "Mighty Atom," a carnival strong man who bent horseshoes with his teeth.

Jim sat on Santa's lap in Hess Brothers Department Store, not really believing in the old guy but still hedging his bets for fear that a bag of coal might be Santa's answer if he displayed any doubts.

My mother often said that Jim had the "devil in him," undoubtedly referring to a combination of his red hair and his impish personality. To put it in terms of a popular TV show of the era, Jim was more Eddie Haskell than Beaver Cleaver.

My mother always believed that Jim was "different" because he was a middle child, as if this position between my sister and me explained everything. But when my mother called him different, she meant it lovingly. My sister and I instinctively knew that Jim was her favorite, and there was a bond between them that my sister and I could neither know nor understand. That bond became clear to us when, after my mother was diagnosed with lung cancer, Jim became her caregiver in a way that my sister and I never could. The way Jim cared for my mother in her last months reminded me of the loving care Jim himself received from Lori and his children before he left this world.

But with Jim, most of all I remember the pranks, endless, juvenile but hilarious pranks, which we simply labeled "goofing" on people. Jim, with his unlimited imagination and craziness, would often push these pranks to the next level and sometimes even over the edge. He was a born trickster, and, as he reached his teenage years, he graduated to the level of bona fide hell raiser. But with his good looks, easy-going smile and charm, he seldom got into any serious trouble.

When he graduated from Dieruff High School, Jim joined the Navy where he served on the biggest and newest aircraft carrier afloat, the John F. Kennedy, commissioned in 1967. We saw little of Jim during those years. He split his time between Norfolk, Virginia, and the Mediterranean Sea. We received letters from Jim from magical-sounding places like Malta, Istanbul Turkey, and countless port cities in Italy, Greece, France and Spain. He saw the world and was gone for six to nine months at a time. When he left the Navy, he lived for years in Clearwater, Florida, and again years went by when our family saw little of him.

I do remember that time in Jim's life when he discovered his faith and started to become the spiritual person he remained until his death. Jim never made a secret of his early struggle with alcohol and drugs, and how the storm clouds had formed for him in his early adult years. At some point after Ryan's birth, Jim realized that he could not be the kind of father he needed to be unless he got clean and sober. He thereafter started the long, difficult journey that turned his life around.

Over time, Jim became an AA success story. Indeed, his commitment to AA's 12-Step Program became a major part of who he was as a person. He stayed clean and sober for the rest of his life and never turned back. And along the way, he found his God and became the best possible father for Ryan. Jim became an AA sponsor for others in need and became a featured speaker at AA meetings and even local colleges. Jim's salvation, however, did not occur overnight. It happened, as Jim often said, "…one day at a time."

More than once, my brother said that Ryan saved his life because his son gave him the inspiration to turn away from the things that were destroying him. With his sobriety, Jim and Ryan became inseparable and the closest of friends. Today, it is plain to see the fine young man that Ryan has become.

By the 1990s, the only thing missing in Jim's life was a good woman or, as they say today, a soul mate. At one point, it seems like only yesterday, Jim called me and announced: "I've fallen in love with a woman from my neighborhood named Lori, and I'm getting married." He told me that Lori was simply the best woman he had ever met, and that she shared the same beliefs and values that he did. He mentioned, coincidentally, that Lori had three children, and they were the three "neatest" kids he had ever seen. With Jim, "neat" was the highest compliment he could pay anyone or anything. He then commenced to tell me, as he did countless times since that first conversation, why each of the three...Candace, Mercede, and Mark... were "neat" or special in their own way. I asked him: "What does Ryan think about sharing you with three other kids?" His response was vintage Jim: "He's getting a great step-mom, and Ryan's tough; he'll adjust to not always being the center of attention."

And the rest, as they say, is history. The best years of Jim's life, without question, have been the ones he spent with Lori and his four children. He did not need to say it. It was obvious from his contentment and the pride in his voice every time he spoke of Lori and the kids.

With Jim, you never had to read between the lines. What you saw was what you got. He had no hidden agenda. He told you what he thought and what he believed in a straightforward way. He was stubborn, but it was a stubbornness borne of his faith and belief in God. For Jim, there were certain absolutes for which there were no compromises.

Jim died at the age of fifty-eight. It is tempting to say that he died too young. But that is not the way Jim would view it. He would tell you that he led a full life by the time his God came to take him, and that he was ready to go. He had decades ago reached out to his God and found a welcoming hand.

For weeks while he lay in his bed dying, Jim was surrounded by the family and friends who loved him. Although the cancer ravaged his body, he was at peace. Each time I would visit him, I left with a sense of awe and wonder at the amount of love in the room with him.

If we reap what we sow, Jim sowed countless seeds of love and devotion during his lifetime. Jim, of course, was loved. But more importantly, he was admired and respected for the valuable life he led, as well as the good he left behind.

Lest we forget,
From his brother.

THE MANY LOSSES OF LIFE

When I am asked to recommend a particular resource for a grieving person to read immediately, I always refer them to the book, *Don't Take My Grief Away* by Doug Manning.

I want to begin this section of my book with this quote about the nature of grief:

Grieving is as natural as crying when you are hurt,
sleeping when you are tired,
eating when you are hungry,
or sneezing when your nose itches.
It is nature's way of healing a broken heart.

As you read the stories shared in this section, you will find that each one speaks of a very unique relationship that existed in their lives. You will also note that grieving is not just reserved for the loss of someone through death. But the fact remains that in order to begin healing, we have to walk "the path of grief." It doesn't always feel "natural," but it truly is "nature's way of healing a broken heart."

SEPTEMBER 11, 2001
Roberta Rudder

I don't like thinking about 9/11, so when asked to write about it, I had to really take a deep breath and think. Sylvia feels it would be good for me to write this essay so I am going to try.

I got on the Transbridge Commuter bus from Allentown to Wall Street that morning like I'd done for over five years. I got into my favorite seat, said my prayers, and settled in. I arrived about 7:35 a.m. I like getting in early. It was a new job, and I'd been there only about three weeks.

Around eight o'clock or so, I went into my manager's office to discuss an account. We were talking when it felt as if something had hit the building. We heard a loud boom, and the building trembled. I was facing the window, and things started to fly. It was paper and what looked like rocks.

I worked at One Liberty Plaza which sat directly across from One World Trade Center. I looked out of the window and saw that the tower had been hit.

"They've done it again," I said. The Trade Center had been bombed in the past.

We were told to leave the building but not to use the elevator. We were told to take the stairs. I grabbed my bag and headed for the stairs. I was afraid I would not make it out of the building. Thank

God I did. I made it to the street and looked up behind me as things were coming out of the tower. I wouldn't look down.

The first thing I remember seeing clearly was a woman in a beige suit flying out of a window. I then realized that what was coming out of the windows were people. I couldn't move. I couldn't believe my eyes. I could see the wing of the plane hanging out of the side of the building. I started praying. I asked God to protect us. I could hear people saying all kinds of things. We were under attack; it was an invasion of the country; and it was crazy.

I couldn't look anymore. I started walking towards a friend's building. Al and I worked in the insurance industry together for over twenty years. His faith was strong. I wanted to get to him. As I was walking, I heard another boom. I looked around and saw the second plane go into the second tower.

When I got to Al's building, I was told he was in One World Trade Center on an appointment. But Chris was there. I told her I had to "get to my kid." She and I started walking back over to Broadway. It was crazy. I remember seeing people bleeding, firemen and policemen were bleeding. People were walking the street mindlessly. As we were trying to get through Broadway, we heard another boom, but this one was different.

I looked around and saw what appeared to be a huge cloud of smoke coming after us. I dropped my bag. We ran up the stairs of what I think was City Hall and asked for shelter, but the doors were locked—and they would not allow us to enter. I remember seeing a woman with a baby in her arms. I asked them to let her in, but they were not permitted to go in. We ran back down the stairs, and there was my bag! I got it. I looked up and saw everyone was covered with this gray dust.

I know that Chris and I were walking, and I remember saying over and over that "...I've got to get my kid." I don't remember how we got there, but we got to a Mission. I remember seeing lots of bleeding people while we were walking. I remember seeing a fireman standing by his truck, and he was covered in blood—and he was crying.

When we got to the mission, they had two "land line" phones working, but there was a long line of people waiting to make phone calls to family. I found a small chapel, went in, and saw an open Bible on the altar. It was opened to the 91st Psalm. I read it and immediately knew that God was with me. Some months earlier, a friend had suggested that I read this Psalm daily. It talks about being protected by the Lord and His angels. How in the midst of any kind of trouble, He will protect me from whatever is going on. When I sat and read it that morning, a feeling of calm came over me. I knew that somehow everything would be okay.

We were asked to leave the mission as there were just too many people there who needed assistance and we were taking up needed space. We walked on and saw a man standing outside his place of business letting people use his phone. It had to be one of the only phones working in the entire area. I called my parents to let them know I was out of harm's way. I also called my daughter, Aminah, who worked on Broadway. Someone took the phone from me and told her where I was. She told me to stand still until she could come to get me. She came, and I was so thankful to God to see her face.

It took me a few days to put together in my mind what had happened. I do know that when I reached my home, I had over twenty-five messages on my machine. I did call most of them back. I couldn't stop crying; I just kept crying and thanking God for my life.

I don't remember when I started getting calls about people who didn't make it out. There were so many. Al was one of them, and the one that hit me the hardest. I know he was trying to save somebody else and that's why he didn't make it. I wonder why God spared my life—and I still do. What is it I am supposed to be doing?

Why them and not me? I keep being told that it wasn't my time.

I am a "recovering alcoholic," and every day I thought about picking up a drink. I kept hearing people screaming. When I closed my eyes, I would see that woman in the beige suit falling out of the window. I stayed very close to my sponsor and the rooms of AA.

Everything happened the way God wanted it to happen. On

September 12, I went to my foot doctor and his assistant knew a Grief therapist she thought I should see. I called and got an appointment immediately. When I reached her, she had already been praying for me because of another connection she had. God was at work.

I have stayed very close to my grief therapist since that time. I check in with her from time to time. I am so sad sometimes. For a long time, my therapist was the only one I could talk to about 9/11. In December I went on "Retreat" and felt safe enough to talk about what happened that day.

September 11, 2001 changed my life forever. I know that there is a God and that He is looking after me every moment of my life. Some days I don't feel it, but I know He's there.

My mother passed away on January 31, 2010. I miss her so much. I have been so depressed and cannot seem to "get it together." So once again, I called upon my grief therapist. She has been wonderful. She tells me that every "new" death stirs up every "former" death in our lives. The depression that one experiences can be deep and very much like a "pit of grief." She also tells me that we have just two things we can control in our lives. One is to consciously decide to change what we are thinking as our thoughts control our feelings. The other choice is to finally reach up for help. It is a choice to come out of the "pit of grief" and to trust that we are being led to a better place.

Roberta Rudder
2012

POSTSCRIPT:

PSALM 91

Whoever dwells in the shelter of the Most High
will rest in the shadow of the Almighty.
I will say of the LORD, "He is my refuge and my fortress,
My God, in whom I trust."

Surely He will save you from the fowler's snare
and from the deadly pestilence.
He will cover you with his feathers, and under his wings you will find refuge;
His faithfulness will be your shield and your rampart.
You will not fear the terror of night, nor the arrow that flies by day,
nor the pestilence that stalks in the darkness,
nor the plague that destroys at midday.
A thousand fall at your side, ten thousand at your right hand
but it will not come near you.
You will only observe with your eyes and see the punishment of the wicked.

If you say, "The LORD is my refuge," and you make the Most High your dwelling,
no harm will overtake you, no disaster will come near your tent.
For He will command his angels concerning you to guard you in all your ways;
They will lift you up in their hands, so that you will not strike your foot against a stone.
You will tread on the lion and on the cobra; you will trample the great lion and the serpent.
"Because he loves me," says the Lord, "I will rescue him; I will protect him,
for he acknowledges my name.
He will call on me and I will answer him; I will be with him in trouble, I will deliver him
and honor him. With long life I will satisfy him and show him my salvation."

New International Version (NIV) Copyright 1973,1978,1984,2011 by <u>Biblica</u>

LOSING JASON
Faye Gery Schuler

I hadn't slept well the night of August 28, 2011, partly because Hurricane Irene was dropping massive amounts of rain on us and the wind was howling. I typically don't sleep well on such nights because I fear waking up with a huge tree from the side woods in bed with me. I was still sound asleep when my husband Ron burst into the room.

"You have to get up! Jason was killed in an auto accident last night!" he screamed.

I couldn't believe my ears. Our wonderful, handsome son-in-law dead! He continued that the police had had trouble finding next of kin because he had not changed his address on his driver's license after he and our daughter Jane moved. They finally located his father, who called Jane. His father was so overcome by grief and disbelief that Jane could barely understand him. Jane and Jason were separated. After the call, she went to his apartment to get their beloved dog Bradley. They were sharing custody of him.

Jason died on his way home to Bradley after visiting friends in this area. Somehow he lost control of his SUV on the Northeast Extension of the Pennsylvania Turnpike. He skidded into and went over the guardrail, down a steep hill, and then hit a telephone pole. State police think be was killed instantly. What really happened? He had driven thousands of miles in all kinds of weather for his job and never had an accident.

Was he driving too fast for conditions and hydroplaned? Was he unable to see in the driving rain? Did the wind play a role? Did he fall asleep? We will never know.

The next few days seemed surreal. Jane was incredibly strong. She put together posters with pictures of his childhood, their time together, and their beloved Bradley. She made up a handout with a picture of Jason "all smiley" on the beach. On the back was a picture of Jason taking Bradley to puppy kindergarten and the following message from Bradley:

Dear Dad,

Thank you for being my dad. Thank you for choosing me out of that entire litter of puppies. Thank you for taking me on walks even when you didn't want to go. And for tolerating all the stops I needed to make just to check things out. Thank you for teaching me about rabbits and squirrels and what fun they are to chase. Thank you for all of those baths you gave me when I had mange and for not getting angry when I shook myself dry instead of using the towel. Thank you for being patient with me at puppy kindergarten. I'm really sorry I was the only dog who refused to wear his hat for his picture. Thank you for giving me head rubs in the elevator. You never missed a beat with those. Just wanted to tell you that I love you and I miss you, Dad.

Your A #1 co-pilot,
Bradley

She even found a cobalt blue (Jason's favorite color) jar and filled it with fortune cookies for funeral attendees. He was definitely a foodie and loved a good Chinese buffet.

So many people came to the funeral—childhood friends, adult friends, family members, co-workers. Everybody liked Jason. Facebook, the funeral home site, and the newspaper obituary site received hundreds of posts. It was unbelievable.

The funeral itself was horrible. After a steady stream of friends and family members had paid their respects and filed past Jason's cremated remains, an elderly deacon of the Catholic Church conducted the service. We were surprised at that because Jason seemed unchurched. And the funeral should have been conducted by a vibrant, young person who knew Jason at least casually, such as the celebrant who married him and Jane, not a total stranger. Unfortunately, the celebrant had another commitment that day. After the service, mourners were invited to speak. Jane talked about how much she loved him and recalled many happy times together. Friends spoke about how much he loved to eat and the good times they had shared. Big, tough guys were crying like babies.

After the funeral a close friend of Jason's told my husband and me that Jason "loved you guys." And his father told us that Jason "thought the world" of us.

After the funeral, we ate fortune cookies. My fortune and my husband's fortune were: "Be calm and collected, peace is a virtue." And "Seize every second of your life and savor it." How appropriate.

We took the funeral flowers back to Suzy's (my other daughter) house. She was having a really tough time because she and a friend were the last people to see Jason alive. We bought dozens of vases at the dollar store and rearranged the flowers in them. Jane planned to deliver them to the hospitals where Jason worked. He liked the part of his job that involved helping people.

While we were arranging the flowers, I asked the girls where they thought Jason was and whether we would ever see him again or be able to communicate with him. Suzy immediately said that he was in heaven with God. Jane, who is spiritual but not a Christian, said she thought he would come back as an insect or a bird. I was indignant at the suggestion that Jason would come back as an insect.

However, later that day when Suzy and I took a walk around her yard, we saw a praying mantis in her flower garden. She had not seen one there for a few years. We joked that it was Jason and laughed to keep from crying. Later when we were leaving Suzy's house to come home, a praying mantis was sitting on the roof of our car! I have never seen a praying mantis anywhere other than on a plant. We joked that Jason wanted to go home with us. But I was afraid it would be injured, and Suzy removed it before we left. The next day Suzy went for a walk and saw two praying mantises.

Because of Jane's comment about Jason coming back as an insect, I decided to look up praying mantis on the internet. I couldn't believe what I found. Here are just a few of the beliefs about praying mantises. The African Bushmen believe that they are a manifestation of God come to earth and that they are associated with restoring life to the dead. In Greek, 'mantis' means prophet or seer, a being with spiritual or mystical powers. In Arabic and Turkish cultures, a mantis points the way to Mecca, the holiest city in the Islamic world. In France, it is thought that the mantis points the way home if you are lost. Also, the praying mantis relates to stillness, quiet, calm, patience, and balance. It does not move until it is certain that its movement is appropriate and, thus, has become a symbol for contemplation and meditation.

A few days after the funeral, I went to my local Garden Club meeting. The presenter was a very spiritual woman who grows one and a half acres of dahlias every year near Hellertown where Jane and Jason had previously lived. Someone asked what she does for pest control. She replied that she has few problems with pests because she has lots of praying mantises! She talks to them and sings to them because she thinks they are a real gift.

Our church family was wonderful through all of this. The pastor offered prayers for Jason, EVERYBODY hugged us, some cried with us, some offered to talk, some offered to help in any way. We got many cards, e-mails, calls, and visits. We had never experienced such an outpouring of love. The ones who knew about the praying mantis didn't even think that I was wacky.

The Labor Day weekend was a difficult time for us. For the past few years we had had a family seafood feast then. We had cold shrimp, fried shrimp, crab legs, steamed clams, and fish.

Last year Jason decided that we needed raw oysters. Apparently, everyone else had decided they needed them too because he went to several stores before finding oysters. He had a difficult time opening them, and then no one really wanted them. I felt so bad for him. I can still see his plate piled high with his wonderful smile and hear him saying, "It's soooo good." We skipped the seafood feast this year.

Around September 8, we experienced another storm—tropical storm Lee. It rained and rained and rained. In fact, Jane had to evacuate her home. Fortunately, her home was not damaged by the floods. It seemed like all of creation was weeping for Jason.

Nothing was being done with Jason's ashes. His father agreed to let Jane have some of the ashes. She selected two containers for them, a small heart and a small urn. The heart she is keeping. The ashes in the urn were to be scattered in the ocean, as Jason had requested. She waited and waited for them and finally they came— by UPS!

I was surprised that someone so young (thirty-nine) would have discussed plans for his ashes. Perhaps it was because Jason had a brush with death several years earlier. His motorcycle skidded out on rough gravel. His arms were injured so badly that they had to be shortened. He had long scars on his upper arms over his elbows and down his lower arms. Miraculously, the skilled surgeons restored his arms to full functionality.

So on October 8, Jane, Suzy, my husband Ron, and I made the difficult trip to the beach (where the "all smiley" funeral handout picture had been taken) to scatter Jason's ashes. Bradley went too. It was his first trip to the beach, and he loved it. It was a beautiful day, and many people were enjoying the beach. First, we bought lunch at a deli (some of Jason's favorite foods including blue potato chips) and ate it in a pavilion.

Because the beach was crowded there, we drove to a residential area to scatter the ashes. We walked through tall beach grasses to get to the water. A few monarch butterflies were in the grasses. I read the Top 10 Things We Can Learn from Jason, which I had written earlier. They are:

10.   Never pass up a good Chinese buffet.

9.   Enjoy the simple things in life—like a peanut butter and jelly sandwich.

8.   Let your final wishes be known.

7.   Work hard.

6.   Take time for fun.

5.   Love deeply.

4.   Live in the moment.

3.   Find pleasure in helping people.

2.   Never grow up completely.

1.   Don't drive in a hurricane.

Bradley dug holes. We took lots of pictures. Then we scattered the ashes. We didn't even know if it was legal, but we didn't care. The ashes were not Jason. They seemed like the ashes from a wood stove.

We walked back through the beach grasses. Now they were covered with HUNDREDS of monarch butterflies! Maybe Jane was right. Maybe Jason had come back as an insect.

We had a lovely dinner afterward and wound our way home the way the GPS told us to go…probably not the best way. It was a difficult day but a good day because we were carrying out Jason's wishes.

Again I went to the internet…this time to look up the meaning of monarch butterflies. My discoveries were surprising. The Chinese believe that a monarch butterfly symbolizes a young man in love. The Japanese think they are representative of marital bliss. The ancient Greeks considered butterflies as the souls of those who have passed away. Butterflies are also thought to symbolize resurrection, transition, celebration, lightness, time, and soul. Overwhelmingly, cultural myth and lore honor the butterfly as a symbol of transformation because of its process of metamorphosis. For Christians, the butterfly is symbolic of our spiritual evolution and of Christ's resurrection and is considered a soulful symbol of our consciousness emerging from a cast-off body. In the western world, the butterfly stands for freedom, fun, and joyous times. It is also symbolizes a state of naturalness and purity.

However, some think that butterflies symbolize transitoriness, as they don't live long.

Since his death, I have experienced Jason's presence a few times. He rings wind chimes when there is no wind; he causes ornaments on the Christmas tree to sway. And Jane experienced Jason's presence through Bradley. He got into bed with her and laid his head on the pillow, which he had never done before. It is as though he was saying that Jason is all right and that they will be too.

And Jane has now had monarch butterflies tattooed on the back of her neck and across her shoulder.

We put off going to the accident site until Thanksgiving Day. It was a dreadful experience. The site had not been cleaned up well. His car's front bumper and headlight were still there. We also found paperwork from his job and fortune cookie wrappers! A friend had attached a memorial to the telephone pole—a cross with his name and birth and death dates—and, yes, a monarch butterfly! She knew nothing about the butterflies at the shore when she made the memorial!

I see them everywhere now – a huge painting of them in a gift shop, in the listing of editors and contributors to Prevention magazine. And I'll bet I will see them and praying mantises this summer again.

When a young person is killed or dies from an illness, one can't help but wonder why. When my good friend died of cancer at age twenty-nine, the minister who did the service said that God needs young people to help him with his work too. But they had so much to live for. And I still can't believe that Jason is dead. I think he will come through the front door flashing that big smile of his and give me a big hug. I guess I will have to wait for that until we meet again in heaven.

It is difficult to find things to be thankful for after such a tragedy. I am thankful that we got to say goodbye to him. After he and Jane separated, he stopped in to thank us for all that we had given them and done for them. I think he truly thought of us as family. He also wanted to say goodbye. Ron told him to keep in touch, but he said he didn't think that would be possible. Prophetic words.

I am thankful that he was killed instantly. He probably experienced little pain. He did not sustain massive injuries and possibly live for years in a vegetative state. I am thankful that he was alone and that it was a one-car accident; no one else was injured or killed. To those who say, "...but he was only thirty-nine," I say, "Yes, but we had him for thirty-nine years."

A few of the good things that happened as a result of Jason's tragic death are that many folks contributed to the American Cancer Society and to the dog rescue group that had rescued Bradley. In fact, they named two puppies rescued shortly after Jason's death Jane and Jason.

A friend sent the following message, "My children received calls this week just because I had to hear their voices." My 88-year-old sister sent, "Somewhere it says that time heals everything. I believe that it is what you do with time that is the healer." And "His paradise came early while ours still awaits us. The Lord must have needed Jason more than we did. When we are finally finished crying, we'll recall all the fun stuff and the good times we shared. And that will be Jason's legacy."

Jane was a bright spot in his life. Their wedding was great fun with everyone in golf carts on a sunny day. Shortly after Jason's death she posted the following on her Facebook page:

> *If only I had known you'd be gone in an instant.*
> *If only I had told you that I loved you more often.*
> *If only I had tried a little bit harder.*
> *I love you.*

Please take some time today and tell at least one person in your life how much you love them."

Faye Gery Schuler
January 17, 2012

THE LITTLE BOY WHO CHANGED MY LIFE
Paulette Kennedy, RN, BSN, NE, BC

"Life can change on a dime."
"You never know what tomorrow may bring"
"Don't let the sun set on your anger."
"Live in the present."

How many times have we heard these phrases? On one very special day in November of 1992 someone very small changed my life forever.

The day began as usual for me. I reported to the PCU to obtain my nursing assignment for my shift. I learned that I was being "floated" to the Transitional Trauma Unit. As I was then a cardiac nurse, I had a great deal of apprehension, even fear when I realized that the "TTU" staff was experiencing an unusual number of staff "call outs" related to illness, and our resources were limited.

I was assigned to the "four bed room." This really raised my anxiety level as I was unaccustomed to caring for four patients with very serious, life-threatening illnesses. As I entered the room and looked around, it was difficult not to notice the little freckle-faced, red-headed boy lying in the bed...so small, so helpless, and surrounded by balloons and what seemed like hundreds of stuffed animals. It seemed like a scene out of the movie, ET,...the one where he was in a closet surrounded by all of the stuffed animals.

His name was Jonathan. He couldn't speak because he had a

tracheotomy. He was so still in the bed, so alone. I cared for my patients, kept them safe, and somehow made it through my shift. The next day, I worked a twelve-hour shift on my own unit. When it was time to go home, I just couldn't leave without going back to TTU to visit the little boy in the bed.

His Aunt was at his bedside. She shared with me that a terrible tragedy had occurred. Jonathan and his family were driving home to an area near the Poconos when they were hit "head on" by a tractor-trailer. Jonathan's father was driving the car and died instantly. His sister and his pet dog were behind the father and in the middle of the back seat. They also died instantly. Jonathan was in the back seat behind his mother. His mother died holding his hand. My heart was breaking for this very small six-year-old boy who had lost his entire family in one cruel moment.

For the next four months, I visited Jonathan every day after work. It wasn't long before he was able to talk with me. We became fast friends. I would bring books in for him to read, and we would draw pictures and share stories. I never asked Jonathan about that terrible night until one day when he drew a picture of his family. I asked him to tell me about the people in the picture. He told me that they were his family and that they lived in Heaven. He also told me that he had four Guardian Angels. He also shared that before his Mommy stopped talking to him, she told him that he should never be afraid because she would always watch over him. His aunt told him that his entire family were now his very special Guardian Angels and would always watch over him. He told me that he could close his eyes and talk to his Angel family any time he wanted to.

I continued my daily visits with Jonathan, sharing some of our stories with my daughters. Jennifer was thirteen, and Lauren was seven at the time. We learned that Jonathan had a favorite football team, the Miami Dolphins. My daughters saved their allowance to purchase a Miami Dolphins Stadium jacket for my new little friend. We all visited him on Christmas day. Through a "friend of a friend" we were able to arrange a telephone call to Jonathan from Dan

Marino, quarterback of the Dolphins. He also sent him a football jersey and a signed football. Jonathan was so excited and so very happy that day.

When the time finally came for Jonathan to be released to his new home with his aunt, I asked my director of nursing if I could have a few minutes to go to the front door with him to say goodbye. When I got to the car, his aunt handed me a little African violet and thanked me for spending so much time with him. I kissed Jonathan on the forehead and made a deal with him that we would write to each other as "pen pals." He promised to draw pictures for me, and I promised to hang them on my refrigerator.

Even though Jonathan left the hospital with bags full of stuffed animals, he had one special friend and his name was "Oscar." "Oscar" was the teddy bear he hugged every night before he fell asleep. Just before Jonathan got into the car, he held Oscar out at arm's length. I kissed Oscar on the forehead.

"No, you took care of Jonathan and now I want you to take care of Oscar," Jonathan said.

My eyes welled up but my heart would not allow me take the one remaining special possession that this little boy had to take to his new life and his new home. His aunt indicated that I should take Oscar home with me. I lovingly held that little bear tight in my arms as that brave little boy got into the car and waved to me until I could no longer see him.

Jonathan sent me many pictures and many letters through the years. He has graduated from college and has had a happy life. He continues to write to me to this day.

And Oscar can be found sitting on my bed each morning. He still receives a kiss on the forehead each night before I go to sleep. You see, Oscar is our very personal connection.

One day…and one little boy…can absolutely change your life!

Paulette Kennedy

Paula J. Hoffman
"How I Wish I Had Known You"
Sylvia Silvetti Havlish

When I knew that I would be gathering stories from my former clients, family and friends for my book, I put the word out that I was hoping to find really special stories to share with others. My good friend, Diane Tollinche, sent me a copy of the obituary of her friend, Paula J. Hoffman, along with a story Paula had written a year before and this note:

"Hi, Syl...This is my friend, Paula. We have known one another since 1970! She was a beautiful person and where she is now, she is in the presence of angels and the Living God! Enjoy (her writing) and let her words administer grace to you. Diane"

OBITUARY

Paula J. Hoffman, 57, of Slatington died on November 18, 2011 at the Hospice House of St. Luke's in Lower Saucon Townwhip. Wife of Gene L. Hoffman they were married 38 years on April 28. Paula was born in Allentown, daughter of the late Malcolm I and Marilyn E. (Schlegel) Davidson. She was a housewife and home-schooled her own children until their high school years. She was a Sunday school teacher at Bethany Wesleyan Church in Cherryville. Survivors: Children Jesse, Bradley, Gregory, husband of Diana and Emily; five grandchildren, Tyler, Madison, Gabriella, Brennen and Briana; brother Al Davidson husband of Darlene, sisters Barbara Clark, wife of Jerry; Joanne Blose, wife of Randy, Charlotte Primrose wife of Chip and Beverly Ault, wife of David.

The obituary went on to give the usual dates and times of services. It was when I turned the page and saw the following letter which Paula had written exactly one year before that I knew what a special and hope-filled story this would be. Here is her "letter" to her friends and family in its entirety:

A WRITING BY PAULA HOFFMAN

November 25, 2010

A HAPPY THANKSGIVING is a certainty to all who live in gratitude to our most generous God. It matters not that our finances might be stretched for or that our resources are diminishing. Our focus need not be on the economy or the empty promises of legislators or businessmen. Our thankful hearts should not be measured by the feast spread out on our tables or the possessions we own. Although poor health, a physical or mental handicap or chronic pain may challenge our resilience and tempt us towards despair, we are still capable of experiencing God's goodness. Our desire for intimacy, to be relational, respected, recognized and received, is integral to being human. Even in the midst of broken relationships, hearts crippled by cruel words, minds shattered by broken dreams or families stressed by desertion, physical or emotional, we can truly rise from the volcanic ash and be thankful.

You see, Thanksgiving is an attitude, a personal choice. It is the natural overflow of intentionally looking for the good, the beautiful and the intrinsic value of creation. It is then allowing the created cosmos to draw our attention to the Creator. If we ponder the grandiose splendor of the night sky, the wonders of nature, the purity of the birthing of new life or the mysteries that lie within a microscopic cell, we can ask with David, "What is man that Thou art mindful if Him or the Son of Man that Thou visiteth Him?" (Psalm 8) The God who is and is able to imagine, design, create and speak into existence such an amazing world, who is magnanimous, magnificent and mighty is also indescribable and awesome. He is also and always will be LOVE.

His love brings us mercy and grace in the life and death of His Son. His love comforts through our most trying moments. His love never tires and never quits. His love is bigger than our biggest crisis. His love whispers to our hearts during a night of pain and uncertainty. His love speaks to us through the din and distractions of life. His love reaches into the very core of our being and our response is gratitude. "THANK YOU."

Happy Thanksgiving to family and friends from one whose heart is bursting with thankfulness.

Love, Paula

I was whispering a prayer of gratitude for the fact that my friend, Diane, shared this beautiful letter with me. But what I read on the last "attached page" from Diane was the crowning piece. Diane had attached a copy of the St. Luke's Hospice newsletter which had featured Paula's story and ended with an incredible poem written by Paula. Once again, here is the entire article from the newsletter. I offer it to you for your thought and your inspiration. Here it is:

HOW CAN I SAY GOODBYE?

A devoted wife and mother, Paula Hoffman's priority has always been to care for her family. Last fall, when Paula's cancer symptoms brought her to St. Luke's Hospice House, her biggest worry was how her illness would affect her family. Paula herself was no stranger to St. Luke's Hospice House. She had sat vigil many evenings when her own mother was a patient there.

"I woke up in the bed at the hospice house and thought... this is what my mom must have felt like, only now it is my family surrounding the bed."

Under the expert care of St. Luke's Hospice team, Paula was able to gain enough strength to return home to the house she loved. Receiving hospice care at home, Paula has been able to thrive and reach many goals that she longed to achieve before she leaver her family behind.

"Our family had been through so much. It has been hard for them to see me at the brink of death. I wanted more than anything to reach out to them with words of comfort and to let them know that I was still here and I needed and wanted them to be near. So I wrote a special poem that I hoped would touch their hearts. I wanted them to know that even though I am dying, I am still living and I need them." By sharing her poem, it is Paula's hope that others will gain greater insight into a hospice patient's perspective.

I want to thank Paula's husband, Gene, for allowing me to include Paula's story and her beautiful poem in this book. If there is anything that expresses the core purpose of my book...to encourage all of you to live now...in these precious present "moments like this," it is Paula's poem. Thank you Diane, Gene and most of all, Paula!

Sylvia Silvetti Havlish

How Can I Say Goodbye?

I see the way you look at me
with questions in your eyes
I feel the words you never say and then I realize
that you're afraid to speak the words,
the ones we know are there.
Those words that pound within our heads
that taunt and tease and scare.
I see the way you turn away
to find something to do.
Perhaps this will all go away
without the storms that brew.
But, no matter what we do or say
the time is coming…true
when I will close my eyes, alas,
and bid you all "adieu."
So speak the words and listen close
for love is in the air;
laugh and cry along with me…
this precious time we share
will all come back as memories
to comfort and to guide
those precious final moments
when I must say goodbye.

Paula Hoffman, 2010

POP...MY BEST FRIEND
Norman R. Havlish

He used to say, "This place is going to kill me." And by damn, it did.

Our friendship began in 1974 where we both worked. Terry and I worked together for more than eighteen years. The bond that we built over those years was the basis of a great friendship. Many times it felt as if we were brothers.

Terry was a gentle soul, very perceptive, and an excellent judge of character. He was a caring and loyal man as evidenced by his daily phone call to his father. He just wanted to check in and make sure that his dad was okay. He always addressed his father as "Pop." One day a very sarcastic and jealous co-worker of ours heard Terry talking to his dad once again and started to call him "Pop." It was meant to be a "slight" to my friend, but he and I decided it was a compliment. I called him "Pop" for the rest of our time together.

Terry would not only talk to his beloved father every day, but each September I would accompany him to his dad's home so we could make sure that his fishing boat was covered and that his home was winterized. It meant so much to me to be asked to join Terry in these "chores of love" as I had lost my own father so many years before that.

The main part of Terry's life revolved around his wife, Linda, and his two step-daughters. Linda was Terry's high school sweetheart, and he adored her. I know that Terry worked diligently to help his two daughters through college, and he was so very proud of their accomplishments. The love and welfare of his family was always his first priority. He was adamant when he would say that "…no one can mess with my family." He meant it!

"Pop," as I lovingly referred to him, loved to hunt and to fish. He and his cousin, Pete, built a cabin in Potter County, Pennsylvania, and he referred to it as his "little piece of heaven." He was a hard worker both at the job and at his home. He loved listening to Penn State football games while he worked on the yard at home. He was a graduate of Penn State and then he joined the National Guard. I remember him making several trips a year to buy one hundred pound bags of bird seed to take to his cabin…to care for his feathered friends.

Over the eighteen years we worked together, the relationship that developed between us was incredible to me. He taught me so much and was very supportive of me. He always defended me when some of the other co-workers were questioning a decision I had made or were complaining about something. He was always highly respected at our workplace, and most people would never question a decision he made. He always gave me good advice and took me under his wing to guide me. Again, he was one of best friends in every sense of the word that I have ever had.

In 1990, I moved to a different division of our company, and I remember Terry advising me not to make the move. For whatever reason seemed to be right to me at the time, I didn't listen and lived to regret it. In 1992, I was downsized from that position and from the company after twenty years of service. I was devastated and knew that I would have to "re-invent" myself and start all over again. Once again, Terry came to my assistance.

We would meet each other every Monday evening and dine together. I cherish the memories I have of those evenings and looked forward to Terry's company and his advice. He truly was like a "big brother" to me.

I was not the only one to be downsized in that year from the company, and as happens many times in these situations, Terry was feeling the stress of having to do the job of three people. The downsized positions were naturally not filled, and the remaining employees were under incredible stress. In the year 2000, Terry told me that he was really considering retiring to ease his stress. This was another time he said that he felt that "...this job is going to kill me."

On July 10, 2001, I was to meet him for lunch. Something came up at my new job, and I couldn't leave for lunch. I knew I could just call Terry later and explain and see him at another time. When I arrived home from work that afternoon, my wife met me at my car and informed me that "...we have to go to the doctor." She seemed very upset, and I assumed something was very wrong with her. I immediately got in her car, and we started for the doctor. I was beginning to worry that the doctor was going to give me "bad news" about my wife as she was very evasive.

When we arrived, she took my arm, led me into an exam room where my doctor and a nurse were waiting for me. It was then Sylvia told me that Terry had collapsed at work and died instantly. I was in shock, didn't believe this news, and then burst into tears. She had been so worried that I would also "collapse" at this devastating news that she had arranged to tell me with my doctor present. They all surrounded me and tried to comfort me.

I felt like a huge part of "me" was taken away. Now there was a big void in my life that could not be filled with anyone else. I couldn't imagine my life without Pop...without my best friend.

Terry was so much more than just a "work friend." He was my mentor, my counselor, my buddy, and my confidant. I thank God every day for the time I was granted to have Terry as my friend.

Rest in peace, Pop. I know that you are now residing in heaven with your mother and father. I know that you are in God's hands. I still miss you after all these years, and I will love and admire you forever. Until we meet again, my friend...rest well.

Norm Havlish
January 2012

TAMMY AND AL...
A FAMILY OF CHOICE
Douglas R. Fay

The following letter was shared with me by a wonderful woman who I met in a Pet Bereavement group this past fall. Tammy came to my group overcome with grief at the loss of her beautiful dog, "Gucci." As happens in so many cases, one death brings up the suppressed feelings and hurt of a previous loss. In Tammy's case, her losses began very early in her life...and were really brought to a crescendo by the loss of her sweet dog.

As she tried to explain a short version of her "life story," it was evident to me that Tammy was coming to grips with some very devastating events. Her friend, Doug, allowed me to share this letter written to an attorney who was helping Tammy in a serious legal matter. I believe that from this letter, the reader can see how our losses can accumulate and have devastating outcomes in our lives. Both Tammy and Doug agree that if this little "insight" into her journey of grief will help even one person to keep on going, then it is worth the glimpse into Tammy's private life. I thank Tammy and Doug for risking the opening of these wounds by trying to help others. Tammy's legal case is now over, and her attorney assured her that it was now appropriate to be able to share this personal letter. I have copied it exactly as it was written by Doug to Tammy's attorney, Don. It follows.

Dear Don,

I met Tammy on July 14, 2005 about seven months after my wife left me for another man. Her smile and bubbly personality were in the background infectious. Her son Shawn and my son Anthony were high school friends and would see each other from time to time after graduation. When we started to date, everyone thought it was great, including me!

At the time we met Tammy had her own cleaning business. It was not a glorious job by any means. She worked hard, literally on her hands and knees. From time to time I would come and see her and she would be scrubbing someone's bathroom floor. It was like Cinderella. Time and time again I told myself that I wanted this to end for her. But, with my divorce I was in no position to help anyone and together we just persevered.

Tammy had several elderly customers when we first met. She had a knack with them because she was so kind and considerate. They loved her and she loved them. I do not say that lightly. There was a bond. One of her oldest customers was at a local nursing home. She had ambulatory problems and obviously had troubles getting groceries. Tammy, without wanting any remuneration, would get her groceries and carry them to her room and just sit with her and talk. Tammy wanted me to meet this woman and on the day I was supposed to go, something came up and we had to reschedule. No big deal, right? Wrong. The next week she passed on. Tammy cried and cried. If you mention her name, she cries.

Why is Tammy so emotionally tied to older people? At age 12 her father died of a massive heart attack. She and her younger sisters were then exposed to a convicted child molester, for whom her mother left her family prior to her dad's death. After an attempted sexual assault, Tammy's older brother took her into custody at age 14 at the Marine base where he was stationed.

With no mother or father in her life, Tammy was a lost and frightened teenager who tried to make the best of a "bad hand" in life.

She did not turn to drugs or alcohol as some people do. Then through very difficult times she managed to raise three sons who all love her very much and appreciate the long and difficult road she has traveled.

One case that will explain Tammy's relationship with her cleaning clients is the story of Maxine and Ray. They were both in their 80's and they loved Tammy as she loved them. She would do anything for her customers except windows! Her motto was, "You have to do your own windows." But knowing Maxine and Ray were too old to handle that, she would do their windows and never charge them an extra penny. It is just the way Tammy handled older people. I was so fond of her for this quality.

A year after I met her she received a call from Maxine. The housekeeper of her neighbor, Al Zeky, has passed away and he needed someone to clean his home. Tammy was often referred by her existing customers because of their absolute trust in her. I remember her saying that she had just met a sweet old man whom she had decided to take on as a new client. At this time, it seemed he would just be another one of her elderly clients.

At the end of the day, Tammy and I would share the events of our day. On the days that she attended to Al's house, she would tell me how nice he was and how terribly lonely he was. Tammy told me how sad she was that the main person in Al' life, his lovely Gracie, was an Alzheimer's patient in a nursing home. Although she had never met Gracie at that time, Tammy was so touched by Al's situation and spent many hours just listening to his stories. He told her of the time he spent in the Army during World War II and how much he loved the Yankees. Their friendship grew.

About a month later, Tammy proudly showed me a candy dish that Al had given her. She said, "I told him that I could not take it, but he insisted that I must." So, to keep him happy, she took the dish and placed it in her cabinet. About two weeks later, he gave her a large salad bowl. It was on top of a "tripod" and she was not sure where to put it. Today she proudly has it in her dining room as a remembrance of Al.

Then in September of that year, Al wanted to help Tammy financially. He told her that she should not have to shoulder so much debt as a single mom and told her that he and Gracie always paid cash for everything. Tammy wished that were the case in her life, but credit was a fact of life for this struggling mom. He insisted to Tammy that he wanted to pay off one of her credit cards and although she resisted and said she could not allow him to do that, he was insistent. He told her that she was like the daughter he and Gracie never had and he wanted to do this for her.

I remember the day as if it were just yesterday when Tammy and I got together and she was crying in gratitude. She said that Al had paid off her credit card and she could not believe that anyone could be so kind and so generous. She was incredibly appreciative of this act of kindness and their friendship grew as she thought of him as the father she had lost so long ago.

Tammy was concerned about his health and the fact that he lived alone. What would happen if he fell at night? The only person who saw Al on a consistent basis was Tammy. Once every three months, Al's elderly niece and nephew would take him to visit Gracie. But other than the two relatives, Al had no visitors. Tammy called "Life Alert" and had a system set up in his house which included a "necklace" to be worn by Al for him to activate in case of an emergency. He wanted Tammy to be his "emergency contact." She agreed, of course.

As time went by, Al wanted to do more and more for Tammy. He told her that he wanted her to think of him as her father and asked her if he could think of her as his daughter. Tammy was elated and wholeheartedly accepted. It was truly a magical time in her life. From that point on, Al's generosity towards Tammy and her children was legendary. He visited her in her row home and quickly made arrangements to improve her living conditions. He paid to have her basement refinished and her old furniture replaced. It was a dream-come-true when Al came over to see it upon completion and he was so happy to have helped her this way. Once again, Tammy was extremely grateful to this honorable man.

Naturally, Tammy and her family spent Thanksgiving and Christmas of 2006 with Al. If it were not for them, Al would have spent those holidays alone. He became a grandfather to her sons and he loved that role. Displayed proudly on the fireplace mantle is a photo of Al with Tammy and her boys and her granddaughter. Al was so happy to have family in his life and it was at that time that he approached Tammy about wanting to adopt her and make it official.

He had his attorney begin the proceedings for adoption. His attorney helped Al to choose a lawyer who specialized in adoption. All the attorneys met Al and could see that this relationship was genuine. Al longed for a daughter. Tammy longed for a father. It was incredible that fate would have their paths cross. I prefer to think of it as "Divine intervention."

As the years passed, Al happily showered Tammy with anything that he could think of that would make her life easier or just make her smile. The gifts to her included a Cadillac Escalade which she had only ever dreamed about. This fine gentleman looked happier than she was on the day he surprised her with that car. To this day, that car represents Al to her and many times I look over to see her fighting back tears. "I miss him so much," she cries. "I still cannot believe all the beautiful things he did for me." I like to remind her that what she did for him at the end of his life was a beautiful thing, too. The last two years of his life were filled with a joy he never thought possible. Instead of being completely alone, he died with a daughter and his grandchildren by his side.

When I think of the relationship they shared, I can only shake my head at the incredible journey they lived. Al and Tammy represent to me two of the most giving people on the face of the earth. Al did not just give Tammy material things he gave her life and faith. He helped to make her "whole." She felt a father's love for the first time since her dad died in 1970. She gave Al many gifts of unconditional love. There are no less than fifty people from construction workers to doctors to lawyers who witnessed the fairy tale. Many saw how devastated Tammy was when Al died and how to this very moment she cries at how much she misses him. So many have related to us how many times they saw Tammy go way "above and beyond" her duties when Al would have an "accident" or there would be some unpleasant job to be done. She did it with love…as a daughter would do. He would tell her again and again, "I don't know what I would do without you." Tammy would simply reply that they were blessed to have each other.

Don, I know that you have a good idea about what is going on with Tammy, but no one except her sons and me can know the devastation she is going through because of these false accusations about her relationship with Al. She has lived with immense depression and lost sleep because of these legal attacks by other people. Tammy also feels that she has let Al down. The only promise that she has been able to keep is to sit and visit Gracie at least twice a month. Tammy goes to her religiously with love and affection. If you look at the "visitors' log" you will see that no one else ever comes by to visit Gracie. Gracie loves the milkshakes that Tammy brings to her and she especially responds when Tammy tells her that she loves her. Tammy does this for one reason only…because she loved Al and she loves Gracie.

And Gracie isn't the only one she visits. She cannot and will not let Al go. The grief of his death and his memory are on her mind every waking hour. She needs a sleeping pill to finally sleep by four a.m. and then she's up and once again feeling the pain of loss. The void in her life that he filled from the moment they met until he passed away on April 12, 2008 is deep. She goes to the mausoleum where he rests and she talks with him at length. She truly believes that he is listening and watching over her. She tells him about her visits with Gracie and how she cannot wait until he and Gracie are reunited in heaven. It is then, Tammy believes, that for the first time, Gracie will be able to recognize and appreciate what comfort and joy Tammy brought to her beloved husband as his adopted daughter. She prays that Gracie will approve and I, of course chime in, "of course she will!"

Respectfully submitted,

Douglas R. Fay

Good Days, Good Moments, Cherished Memories
Patti Merlo

Although we thought we were prepared for the inevitable, we found that nothing can prepare you for the painful emptiness that follows losing a beloved pet. My husband and I had been talking about the possibility of getting a dog in 1996 but never expected it to be "love at first sight!" Our journey with Belle began one Friday evening while we were shopping at a local mall. We stopped briefly at a pet store "just to take a peek!" But, after only about two minutes with this sweet Basset Hound whose beautiful eyes melted our hearts, we took her home.

As the years passed, we were introduced to people who would become very important in our lives. It started with the veterinarian, Dr. John, who won our hearts when he greeted Belle just one week after we brought her home. Our long and trusting relationship with him has been a journey of hope. Her instructor at the obedience school also helped us to decide to train Belle as a therapy dog. He said that nothing "fazed" this dog. He was right! She was the perfect animal for therapy. She had the perfect temperament to share her unconditional love of the lives she touched. She was given an Animal Hall of Fame award by the New Jersey Veterinary Foundation for the work she did at the Liberty State Park Family Center after the September 11th disaster.

When Belle was five years old, we decided to add another basset to the family. Heidi came to join the fun. At first, Belle wanted nothing to do with her but before long they became inseparable. When Belle was about eight years of age, she had to have surgery for a slipped disc in her spine. We were vacationing in Florida for my husband's fortieth birthday when we were called about the injury. We ended our vacation immediately and headed back to our home in the middle of the night. It was our way of repaying her with the same unconditional love that she gave to us. Although it was a risky surgery with unknown results, she pulled through and was walking just a few hours after surgery. She had won her first major battle.

As time went on, we knew our journey with Belle was getting shorter since the average life span for a basset hound is ten to twelve years. When she reached age thirteen, I decided that I should start to prepare myself by reading a book, Saying Goodbye to the Pet You Love. But there is really nothing that can prepare you for the raw feelings that occur. After all, we had no children, and Belle and Heidi became our "children" in every way. Belle had the usual medical maladies that occur in an aging pet including some cysts, urinary tract infections, and some bouts with colitis. But we noticed one day that she wasn't herself, thinking it was her arthritis. We had x-rays taken of her neck. They accidentally discovered a spot on her lung that didn't look good. We decided with the doctor that at her age the risk was too high for a biopsy. If she did have a tumor, surgery would not be recommended. It was the beginning of some tough decisions.

Just before her fourteenth birthday, she developed a condition known as "Old Dog Vestibular Disease," otherwise called "vertigo." Just when we thought Belle was "back to normal," it was discovered that Heidi had auto-immune hemolytic anemia. We felt it may have been caused by the rabies vaccine she had received just two weeks prior. And just to make things interesting, my husband developed Bell's Palsy and a MRSA infection in his foot. He was on bed rest for five weeks. It is a wonder to me that I didn't end up in a padded room! I just learned to take things one day at a time.

2010 was a very tough year for Belle; for us it was when the good years turned into good months. Belle's medical issues were increasing. She developed pancreatitis which was treated with fluids administered beneath her skin, an abscess in her mouth causing her eye to get "puffy" and atypical Cushings disease. With so many doctors' appointments it felt like we had our own revolving door. Although Belle had started to lose weight, through it all she never lost her personality or spunk. We had a few conversations with the veterinarians on knowing "when is when," and they always concurred there was still life and fight in Belle's eyes. Our hearts were being torn apart watching her age so quickly.

The week before Labor Day her pancreatitis acted up again, and she had to once again go in for "sub-q" fluids. She seemed to rally over that weekend, and we were certain we could cancel the appointment we had for the following Tuesday. However, her eye was looking "puffy," and we went in to the appointment feeling that she would get more antibiotics and recover again.

We were not ready for the doctor's words that morning. Belle was very quiet when they took her temperature. It was 103 degrees. Dr. Lori took one look at Belle and said, "I think it's time."

Although we were expecting to hear those words "someday," we were not prepared that day.

After some discussion, Dr. Lori asked us, "Is she having good days or good moments?" The answer put it all into perspective, and we realized that it was time for us to help our little girl to make her final journey over the Rainbow Bridge.

We took Belle outside in the sun and sat on the grass for a while just loving her. We told her how much she meant to us, thanked her for being in our lives, and told her how sorry we were to say goodbye. I have some regrets that I didn't just take her home and lavish her with all the things she loved that she was deprived of because of her condition. However, we knew that it was now time to let go.

They brought us into a room. Bob sat on the bench, and I sat on the floor holding her. Rocking her as I used to do when she was a puppy when she would fall asleep in my arms, only I knew this would be the last time. It wasn't easy, but I was determined to be strong and not let her sense how upset I was. Dr. Lori was wonderful and explained everything as it proceeded.

By the time it was over my twenty-nine pound basset hound felt like a heavy weight in my arms. It was a very strange sensation to literally feel the life just disappear from her body as Bob watched the life disappear from her beautiful eyes. I held her for a little while longer, and then the techs came to take her…but not before one last kiss on her head and a last "I love you."

As we left the office, the entire staff was offering us their sincere condolences through their own tears. Belle had made an impact on everyone. We received a chrysanthemum from the vet's office about an hour after we got home. It was then that the emptiness started to hit us.

I spent the next few evenings putting together a "picture tribute" of Belle's life. It was very therapeutic and helped to ease a tiny bit of the pain I was feeling

Over the next few weeks, I began to feel guilty and was questioning if we did the right thing at the right time. During that time I saw four rainbows. The first one was actually on the day Belle was cremated, and the last one was a "double arch." I honestly think it was a sign from Belle telling me to stop worrying because she made her journey across the "rainbow bridge" and that she was okay!

We started noticing that Heidi was also "grieving" the loss of Belle. We noted that she seemed depressed, and our veterinarian recommended a flower essence to try and amazingly it helped to soothe her mood. We eventually added another basset to our family when Abigail arrived six months after Belle died. No animal could ever replace our Belle, but Abigail has helped to ease the pain for both of us and for Heidi.

One of the things I have learned from our experience and from taking part in a Pet Bereavement group offered at Valley Central Pet Referral Hospital is that it is normal to express our true feelings about our loss. In the group I have met other "pet parents" who totally understand our feelings and we help each other through this path of grief. By realizing our pain can be a comfort to others suffering the same loss, Bob and I have been able to offer helpful advice to our friends who have recently lost their faithful companions.

Since losing Belle, I never know what will trigger a memory. The smallest thing could start the tears flowing...a photo, an event, something Abigail does that we forgot Belle had done. We still have our moments of sadness, but at least now we can shed tears of joy over the good thoughts of her life with us. We were blessed with almost fifteen years together and thank God for every precious moment he allowed us to share with her. Belle took her place of honor among all the other shining stars in the night sky, and I believe she will meet us again at the bridge when our time comes. The painful memories are always there, but the good moments slowly turned to good days, then good weeks and good months. We are working on the beginning of a good year, and most importantly, we have a lifetime of cherished memories of Belle.

Patti Merlo
January, 2012

GREAT GRANDMA, ANGIE KRAUSE
Colleen Krause-Straw

As I was growing up, I was very close to my great grandmother. She was a part of my life every day until she passed away when I was just twenty-three years old. She told me stories of our life together beginning when I was a baby and she lived next door to us. She said that she would hear me crying in the middle of the night and would walk over and knock on the door to take me to her home, rock me to sleep, and give my parents some rest.

She was a wonderful woman, and people would fall in love with her the minute they met her. I spent many hours with her in her home just watching television or eating dinner with her. We liked to watch her favorite soap opera, General Hospital, in the afternoon and she watched the Lawrence Welk Show in the evening. I remember her sitting in her dining room window and watching for me when I came home from school. I had great private times with her talking about everything…from how she married my great grandfather to telling me to stay away from the boys! We were the best of friends.

She showed me how to cook and bake some of her favorite meals, and I helped to rewrite her old cookbook. Her handwriting was becoming "wobbly" so she liked my writing better. I loved these times with her.

I remember watching the moon walk with her and asking her, "What is it like for you to have grown up with a horse and buggy, and now you're watching a man walk on the moon?" She never drove a car, but she was intrigued with the idea of men walking on the moon. I was fascinated with our family history, and she filled me with many stories. The last time I spent with her, I was at her bedside and shared with her that I had just become engaged. It was our secret. I wouldn't tell anyone else until I had that ring on my finger. Her health was failing, and the doctor came to her house and said she needed to go to the hospital.

The very next day after I shared my secret with her, my parents drove her to the hospital. I was there to help her into the car. My very last words to her were that I was sure she would be fine and that I would come to see her after she was admitted to a room. She never made it into a room because upon her arrival in the emergency area, she had a heart attack and was gone.

It was an extremely sad time for me because she was like a mother to me. I think of her everyday and have a picture of her on my bookshelf next to my bed. I believe she is watching over me. A few years ago, I awakened in the middle of the night from a vivid dream. In the dream, my great grandmother, Angie, came to me and told me how happy she was about the changes in her home. She showed me the beautiful new green kitchen cabinets. When I stood at the sink, where I spent many times getting a glass of water, I realized I could no longer see her beautiful garden. This annoyed me, as I could still picture her in the garden fussing with the vegetables, but I could no longer see the garden from that window. She drew me away from the window and told me she was so upset that there was a spot on the carpet that she just couldn't get clean. She pointed to the floor under her window in the dining room. She said that every time she thinks it is clean, it just come right back when it dries. We laughed and that was when I woke up.

I felt so strange because the dream seemed so real. I could have sworn that we had been talking to each other. I called my mother in the morning and told her about the dream. She was very curious and told me that the house my great grandmother lived in was now a rental property that she was taking care of. She went to see the tenant and told him about the dream.

He laughed and told her to come in so he could show her something. My mom was amazed to see the newly painted green cabinets. The color was exactly what I saw in the dream. She stood at the sink and also noticed that she could not see out the window or see out into the yard.

Then she asked him about the carpet, and he showed her the stain on the carpet below the window that he could not get clean! She stood in amazement and was speechless. Everything my great grandmother showed me was true and had just happened recently.

Now I know that this may sound strange to hear these happenings, but my grandmother made sure I knew that she was there and was in contact with me. I know there is a heaven and that she is waiting for me. Although she has been dead now for more than thirty-five years, I am comforted every time I look at her picture before I go to sleep. Her face is the last image I see before I sleep...and before I dream again.

Colleen Krause Straw
Jacksonville, Florida
2012

IN THE WOODS
Katrina Fritz

She died in the month that her husband's favorite flowers bloomed. Grammy Dodd had long since given me the beloved red peonies that bloomed in the month of May. When she was eighty, she was still living on her own in the Pocono Mountains, but I would always try to have her come to Allentown to see the peonies. Each time she came, she would marvel at how big, vibrant and robust they were. "They must really like the spot you have them in," she would say, but I knew in my heart that it was because I loved them so because they were from her. When the time came that she was no longer able to keep her own home, I would cut them for her and bring them to her to admire.

You may think that Evelyn Mader Dodd was my grandmother, but in reality, she was my husband's grandmother. I had known her from the time I was fourteen years old and loved her as if she were my own. Grammy Dodd taught me how to sear roast beef to keep it juicy. She told me to make the gravy in the same searing pan, how to add just the right amount of flour to the drippings, and then slowly bring it to a boil so it wouldn't get "lumpy." Grammy also taught me how to make pickled beets which I still prepare for the family every Christmas. Another food-related Christmas memory comes from Grammy Dodd. While my husband and I were still in high school, I remember the adults always receiving a box of her treasured chocolate-covered crackers. I knew that when I had finally received a box of my own, I had truly become an adult! It wasn't long after receiving our first box that she no longer brought her own presents... but we did get one box that we gloated about for many months.

Grammy Dodd taught me how to be strong. She was a widow from a young age, but she still remained by herself in the home that her family had grown up in. She tirelessly worked to maintain her gardens, did the yard work, and cleaned her house. She loved her flowers, and I miss the way she always shared her knowledge. If we walked in the woods, she could tell you the name of any wildflower we found. I still feel closest to her there, in the woods. When I think of someone who was virtuous, I think of Grammy. Truly she was a woman to admire and emulate.

It was so difficult to see such a proud and strong woman declining. Because she had always worked so hard on her own, it was difficult for her to accept help and difficult for us to watch her struggle with accepting the help. After one really bad illness, we convinced her to allow us to bring her to live with her daughters. She would split her time between her daughter in Allentown and the one in Ottsville. She never returned to live in the house that her father had made, but she expressed gratitude for being able to live close to her great-grandchildren. She said that they "kept her young." One of my fondest memories is of watching her sit on the piano bench with my daughter, Autumn, as they shared their love of music with one another.

A few years passed and Grammy became more and more frail. Her spine had compression fractures, and she was in a lot of pain, although she never complained about it. I noticed that she would say that she was really tired and she did less and less. This was not like her at all.

I tried to distract her from her pain by asking her to tell me stories about her life. One of the most romantic stories was about the time she took the train to Tennessee to marry her husband before he was "shipped out" to go to fight in World War I. Whether she could speak much or not didn't matter as the time went on...I just loved being in her peaceful and comforting presence.

When Grammy really started to falter, it was hard on all of us. Her daughter, Kay was especially heartbroken and kept trying to get her to eat and move. One of the last things she ate was a piece of my husband's oatmeal bar, which she loved. I tried to help her get around, but she was just in too much pain—and she didn't want to try anymore.

She made up her mind that she wanted to go with Grandpa Dodd, and now we had to come to terms with that ourselves. Her last days were hard, but so rewarding for us. We spent time singing hymns, reading and just talking with Grammy. Each night I would help my mother-in-law to "get her settled" for bed. She was becoming less and less lucid now. One night my husband noticed that she seemed to be muttering and speaking to someone. When he asked her who she was talking to, she answered, "Jesus, of course!"

I had gone over night after night to see her, and I knew that her time was drawing near. She seemed to be holding on until Rob's aunt could get home. I was so afraid she wouldn't be able to hold on that long. As her time was coming near, I had to leave to take my daughter on her Girl Scout camping trip. I bent close to her on the bed with my cheek next to hers and whispered, "I love you, Grammy. I have to go with Autumn's troop tomorrow…and this will probably be the last time I see you. Know that I love you, and it is okay to go when you are ready. Don't wait for me." Tears were streaming down her face even though she had not been able to communicate for days. It was one of the most poignant moments of my life.

The next morning we woke up in the Pocono Mountains on our scout camping trip. I knew that she was gone before the phone rang to tell me that she had passed after her daughter had called. I could hear her saying goodbye in the rustle of the leaves and the rush of the wind past my face. I had always felt close to Grammy in the woods.

Katrina Fritz
January 16, 2012

Jayme Atiyeh Grimaldi: Your Light Shines On!

Sylvia Silvetti Havlish

The first time I "met" Jayme was on the telephone. She was the daughter of one of my dearest friends, Dottie. My son had just moved to Philadelphia to begin a job search. Jayme was working in Philadelphia then as a human resources professional and immediately volunteered to help him. She called to give me some ideas and her "contact" number to give to Chris, my son. She had never even met us yet in person, but she was immediately ready to help. I have learned that this was the heart of Jayme...a heart filled with love and light.

I will begin my story of Jayme's journey with an article that she wrote just a few weeks before she passed away. She had this copied and sent out to the newspaper and to many others in order to help her precious family after her death. It was called "A Mother's Wish". Here it is:

A Mother's Wish

My name is Jayme Atiyeh Grimaldi. I'm forty-one years old and the mother of two beautiful children. Talya is eight and Jake is six. My husband is Matthew Grimaldi. I was diagnosed with breast cancer in 2005, eight months after the birth of my second child. I had to undergo a double mastectomy and multiple courses of chemotherapy at the age of thirty-six. I was told in the summer of 2006 that I was "cancer free" and remained that way for three precious years.

In the summer of 2009, I was playing "chase" with my then six-year-old daughter, Talya, and four-year-old son, Jake. I slipped and fell and hurt my back. The pain continued to get worse, and after a serious of scans, I was told the breast cancer had come back. This time it metastasized to my bones and this summer, to my liver. Recently we found that I'm losing my battle with Stage Four metastatic breast cancer.

Cancer seems to be a disease that has touched everyone's life in some way. I never imagined I'd be touched by this disease the way I am. After my visit with Hospice, I had to face some tough decisions no one should ever have to make. I'm not giving up hope but what I'm asking for is this wish as a mother and a wife. My wish is to give my family peace of mind, support, love, and financial freedom from my medical expenses.

I'm asking that you please donate any amount to help offset the medical expenses that have incurred. I do this in knowing so many have helped me in so many ways and appreciate all that you have done for me and my family.

Thank you in advance. Also, I ask you to do this: live your life while you can and hug the ones you love every single day.

Sincerely,
Jayme Atiyeh Grimaldi

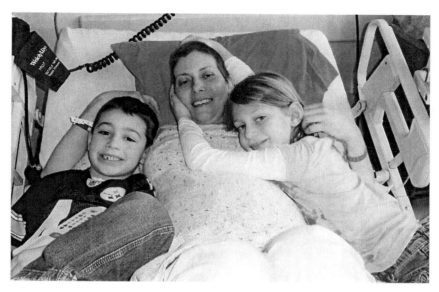

Jayme Atiyeh Grimaldi and her children, Jake and Talya.
One week before her death.

I wanted to write this postscript to Jayme's life to honor her. After I had the opportunity to meet Jayme and get to see her with her mom, her children, and her husband, I knew that I had met an "angel" on this earth. In the midst of her battle with cancer, her mother developed serious blood clots in the lungs. Although Jayme lived two hours north of her mom, she was there in the hospital with her children trying to cheer her mother up. Of course, I learned later that before she arrived at the hospital, she had stopped at her mom's house and thoroughly cleaned and straightened it up for her mom's eventual return. There was nothing that Jayme wouldn't do for her loved ones. She was the most "other-centered" woman I think I have ever met.

During one of her many hospitalizations, I called her and asked if it was okay for me to visit her. She exclaimed, "Oh yes, but please, Sylvia, can you come just a little before my mom arrives? I want to talk with you."

Of course I arrived when she asked me to get there. And what was it she wanted to talk with me about? She wanted to make sure that I would be there for her mom…during this terrible journey called breast cancer. She thanked me first for being such a "good friend" to Dottie…and then held my hand as she talked with me about her love and concern for her mother, her sisters, and her children. As a counselor, I listened but as a friend, my heart was breaking. Not one time did she talk about herself, her fears, or her pain. I was so in awe of her strength, her love, and her courage.

On February 10, 2011, the world lost one of its most precious angels. I know that she now lives as an angel with God in the place where there is no pain and there is no sorrow. We grieve, but not as those who have no hope.

As I read the "guest book" on the newspaper website after her death, I was once again reminded just how many lives this courageous young woman had touched. Her love and graciousness were mentioned by so many people from locations all over the United States. No matter where she lived, the people who met her and knew her were moved to write beautiful memories and express their lasting love for Jayme.

My dear Jayme, your light always shone so brightly during your life and continues to shine on in the hearts and minds of all of us who miss you and love you so much.

Rest now in peace.

Sylvia Silvetti Havlish

THE ULTIMATE LOSS: A CHILD'S BETRAYAL

Diane Rizzetto

It was just before Christmas, a child's favorite time of year when it happened. It was a winter morning when my father went in to work at the printing shop as he had done for years. The day seemed normal until it was lunch time. That's when my life would change forever. My father stood up and asked, "Who would like to have a one and a half year old little girl?" Instantly a young woman stood up and said that her mother would probably take her. They were talking about me. That day my journey of betrayal began.

My father took me to a stranger's house and gave me away as if I were a cat or dog. Since my father had my two older sisters to care for, one of them five years old, the other eight, I was looked upon as an added burden and expense. I was told that my mother would be in the hospital for many years due to her mental illness and would be unable to care for any of her children.

The family I was given to told my father that they were Christians who went to church four times a week and sang in the choir. They did not smoke, did not curse, did not play cards, did not drink alcohol. But, the one thing they did do was to sexually abuse children. I was at the top of their list.

When I was old enough to understand, my foster father told me that I must never say anything about this abuse because no one would ever believe me. Why? Because my mother was in a mental institution, and they would assume that I, too, was unstable. Finally when I was nine years of age, my foster father died. Everyone around me was wondering why I wasn't crying for my "loss." Actually, I was thanking God and even asked him why it took Him so long to answer my prayer. I don't think He ever answered that last question. At least I never heard Him or my ears just weren't listening enough, but my heart was bruised with tears.

In the sixties and seventies it seemed that this type of "problem" was not spoken of openly. I felt I had no one to confide in who would believe me. I felt totally alone in the world.

By the time I was fourteen years old, my biological mother returned and asked me to move in with her. It didn't take long for me to realize that she wasn't completely healed and was still very sick. At age sixteen, my older sister invited me to move in with her and her family, although I would find out later that her family was physically abusive, too. I finally moved in with a high school friend and her family.

It was during this time that my aunt and uncle co-signed a loan for me to get a car, go to cosmetology school, and find a job so I could move out on my own.

After finishing high school and cosmetology school and a taking a few college courses, I finally landed several jobs. It was shortly after that when I met my husband, Jerry. He was a very caring person who listened and seemed to understand where my life had been. Together, we started a new, clean journey. We married when I was twenty years old and eventually had two lovely daughters. The first daughter was born when I was twenty-three and the second when I was twenty-eight years old. We moved to the neighborhood we currently reside in and enjoyed a wonderful life with many new friends and neighbors.

I still wasn't happy with God!

When it came time for our oldest daughter to be confirmed, The Monsignor from our church thought it was also time for me to become a Catholic and share quality family time in church. Soon after I joined the church, Monsignor asked Jerry and me to go on a church retreat. When I said "yes," which surprised Jerry, it was another step that brightened our journey in life.

As our lives progressed, the next step had become darkened with shock, disbelief, and doubt when I was diagnosed with breast cancer at the age of forty. I had a mastectomy and then reconstructive surgery and therapy that went on for years. I enrolled in the group therapy sessions that were suggested by the hospital so that I could discuss MY disease. It was so depressing that I could not keep going to that group. I finally connected with a church group which helped me much more. It was about this time that I met some women who were associated with Mary Kay Cosmetics. As soon as I attended one of their training sessions, I realized that this company was about much more than selling cosmetics. It was truly about women empowering women. I was privileged to meet Mary Kay Ash herself when I attended a company seminar in Dallas, Texas. This association with her and this dynamic group of women really helped me to have a positive attitude once again...and it helped me to put God back in my heart. After several years, I decided that it was time for me to move on and go back to the cosmetology industry. I was able to open my own spa and start giving back to the community by donating hair for cancer victims, donating time and services to other women going through cancer and by giving them hope that there is life after cancer. I know that when you help others, you are being helped yourself in so many ways.

The betrayal that I felt from God, my parents, my foster parents, and the world in general has lessened in my mind as I have matured. I have given God more room in my heart and in my life. In sharing my story with you I hope that when you believe that God has let you down, that you will remember me, then get down on your knees and talk to Him! My prayer is that He will lift you up as He has lifted me.

Love for all...

Diane L. Rizzetto
January 2012

Carole and her Trixie

SWEET DELIVERANCE
Carol Guzy

Trixie was a Special Needs Katrina puppy with twisted legs and neurological issues, but Best Friends Animal Society believed her life had value. They rescued her. Then she rescued me.

At a blessing of the animals here in my hometown of Bethlehem, Trixie was honored. "Oh, Trixie, most divine of God's creation," proclaimed Reverend Mariclair Partee. "We bless you this day as we bless those who have chosen you in this life. We pray that you are delivered from suffering and you stay joyous."

It took place in an ancient cathedral on Wyandotte street where I grew up. I was disappointed to have missed the annual Feast of St. Francis at the Cathedral Church of the Nativity since she was facing a life-threatening illness. Rev. Partee graciously agreed to sanctify my four-legged bundle of blissful Pug-Mastiff mix.

Trixie was born of the hurricane that ravaged New Orleans. Destiny dealt a full-scale challenge to the pint-sized pup. She had malformed legs and neurological tremors that looked like small endless earthquakes inside her. With splints and her own iron-willed fortitude, one paw turned in the correct position, She had the tiny face of an old soul and the essence of an angel but veiled in the rambunctious canine version of a wiggling whirlwind. Her tail swayed endlessly, even thumping the floor in her dreams. Actually her entire body wagged bursting with the unbridled delight of just being alive.

In 2005, she was brought to a temporary refuge set up by Best Friends in New Orleans where for six months as a photojournalist I documented the tragedy and unprecedented animal rescue effort. Her fate may have been different had she gone to a local shelter overwhelmed by the puppy explosion on the deserted streets of the ravaged city. The family who found her had suffered their own hardships, but one little girl insisted her life mattered. She even put Popsicle sticks on those misshapen legs in an effort to make her whole. She couldn't run like other dogs but sauntered with an endearing Charlie Chaplain gait. She played the cards life dealt with grace, gratitude, and dignity.

Her profound resilience of spirit became an inspiration and icon of hope, especially to those with disabilities or adversity. She represented that unique quality in certain beings that allows them to rise above adversity and speak to the best in all of us. Most people who met her initially shed tears but were quickly touched by her tenacity and uplifted by her antics. She possessed a dogged (pardon the pun) determination. She hurtled herself headfirst into your heart.

Though she had "special needs"—most of all she was special. Yet the shelter was closing, and no one wanted her. She wasn't "perfect." Empathy evolves when we realize we're all broken in some way. We drove home the eve of my fiftieth birthday. I had my greatest gift with me. It seemed we had weathered all her storms. But five years later, on my birthday, she started having serious difficulties, signs of a progressive nerve disease that has no cure.

～

On family leave from work to help my ninety-five-year-old mother on her final journey, the possibility of also facing the loss of this beloved furry family member was overwhelming. Add to this, other losses or abandonment, and it created a pervasive ache. Sorrow seems to come in droves, never as a drizzle. It floods your world.

Trixie was only five. You try everything. Specialists. Acupuncture. Holistic herbs. Anger. Worry. Prayer. She, on the other hand, was happy as a clam. She didn't wallow in self-pity, she adapted. When I cried at the sight of her struggling to drag herself across the room, beaming with elation as the food bowl clinked, she consoled me. That's the thing about dogs. They never, ever hurt you. Until they die. And they would spare you that sadness if they could.

Her collar was adorned with daisies from my mother's nursing home garden and pink ribbons, much to her canine chagrin. But my little twisted girl never looked prettier than on that poignant day.

As we left for church, withered sienna autumn leaves floated by darkened clouds reminiscent of an ethereal scene from the *Wizard of Oz.* I later learned my favorite song, *Over the Rainbow,* was played by the choir at the original service. The skies unleashed a deluge of rain, as if all of heaven was weeping for my Trixie.

Overcome with emotion during the brief ceremony in the empty cathedral, I felt waves of gratitude that the sacred stranger in white robes cared about this animal that has given me such joy and made me smile even in the darkest hours.

Trixie peacefully rested her head on my shoulder during the service, her collar now also adorned with a medal of St. Francis. Huge trusting eyes looked up at me and my heart wrapped around her, holding her safe in the divine warmth of this stunning place.

I couldn't fix her—hard as I tried. But I could love her.

We can pray for miracles but accept all there is to hold onto is now. On this day, she was blessed. For the past five years, my blessing has been Trixie.

I will cherish Rev. Partee's soft, poignant words:

"Trixie...We ask that God grant you strength in your suffering and a sweet deliverance from this life when the time comes."

"Amen."

"We who choose to surround ourselves with lives even more temporary
than our own,
live within a fragile circle, easily and often breached.
Unable to accept its awful gaps, we still would live no other way.
We cherish memory as the only certain immortality, never fully
understanding the necessary plan."

-The Once Again Prince

On the afternoon of August 10, 2011, Trixie laid her head on my heart and quietly slipped away. That moment my soul was eternally altered. I'll light a candle this afternoon to mark her passing. One of my gentle friends, who lost her young son years ago, doesn't judge. She believes all grief is equal to the depth of love and deserves respect and empathy. It hurts as much today as it did a year ago. She was my joy and the glue that bound me as I'm losing my only family including both my mother and sister to Alzheimer's, which is the longest goodbye. They're here. But they're not.

There have been so many other losses and abandonment in recent years, but none so profound as this. Why are bonds formed with some that even death cannot unravel? Some would say she was "just a dog." But for me, she was the essence of grace and decency in a furry body. The human species could learn a great deal about humanity from our non-human kin and by letting go of "selective compassion." In journalism we bear witness to the evils of mankind, but also to quiet poetic gestures of courage and kindness that humble us. Yet never have I known a soul as pure as Trixie. Some would scorn mourning a pet, but they are most unfortunate to never know this most special bond.

It's not the anniversaries of grief that are the worst. It's the little moments you least expect: a familiar scent, a memento in a long-unopened drawer, tender thoughtfulness from a stranger. They take your breath away, and the mourning begins anew. Reliving memories of sitting devastated and completely alone with her tiny body last year arise. One friend knew I needed someone to take a leap of faith and mercy. She cancelled work and immediately got on a plane that day to help as I collapsed in anguish. Initially there is support— cards, flowers, cherished gifts, daily phone calls to keep you from the edge. But as time passes, many naturally move on with their busy lives. Yet those in grief remain mired in despair. We try to function and work in a world now darkened. We try to maintain strength when caregiver fatigue and more impending farewells have worn us raw. The waves continue to wash over us, and we tread water, so as not to drown in a sea of sorrow. But there is solace in memorial tributes like this and keeping a journal of memories, the images that time eventually steals from our recollection.

Long ago, others didn't see past her disabilities to a radiant spirit that brought delight to all. I would not trade all the tears of this year for one moment of that time with her. But today I sit alone again with the emptiness. Even the skies are weeping again on this anniversary day, and the winds are blowing, making my chimes ring a sweet song.

For a brief while I was able to hold an angel. Now heaven holds her.

~

Angel's Rest at Best Friends is a magnificent spiritual place in the canyons of Utah with over nine hundred wind chimes. Trixie offered unconditional love to all. I asked everyone to spend a moment thinking about Trixie or lighting a candle during her remembrance service there, so that her gentle essence might feel it and know that she, too, was loved. Please accept my sincere gratitude to all for your deep compassion by honoring this request.

For humans we have funerals, and people gather from far and near to pay respects and offer consolation and closure. It's different for pets, but the grief is no less intense. I never loved anyone more in my life than that little dog, as much as any parent loves a child. She slipped away too soon. There are regrets. If only I watched over her more closely this time, if only I was the medical advocate our loved ones need when they have no voice. If only...

The day began with the moon setting over the red rock canyons. It was a very warm, still day until moments before the ceremony began. Then the winds began to rage, and the nine hundred wind chimes at Angel's Rest started ringing loudly. At first I was upset because I couldn't hear the prayers, especially for the video keepsake.

My friend who works there said that during a placement of an animal, there are always a few chimes that softly ring, but never so powerful as this. With her spiritual wisdom, she said I was missing the bigger picture. It felt as if all the energy everyone was sending into the universe at that moment was reaching Trixie's spirit to let her know she was so very cherished. And this was a sign from her to acknowledge that gift. It's as if her tail was wagging so hard, it created the winds making such a poignant and moving melody. As the ceremony ended, so did the wind.

We placed her plaque and exquisite rock painting near the Katrina memorial, which has markers in the shape of an arc to represent a rainbow. A lock of her fur is now part of the sacred ground. Her St. Francis medal and tiny crystal hearts lay on her marker as the sun reflects rainbows from them onto the words of farewell on her plaque.

Crows and others birds passed overhead. It seemed they were also bidding her goodbye. It is a place where literally, as in the song, "blue birds fly." As the sun set, purple candles flickered and I played *Somewhere Over the Rainbow.* Now her spirit has gone home

A few days later a double rainbow appeared over Angel's Rest.

While at Best Friends, I received sweet kisses from Minka, a special needs dog that I almost adopted. She is now part of the "Guardian Angels" program to which we contribute for extensive medical care they provide. Minka's twisted legs are reminiscent of Trixie's. For those of us who believe disabilities do not define anyone, her life also has worth.

As a photojournalist I've witnessed evil, at times on a massive scale. We humans could learn a lot about humanity from our non-human kin. We've seen that "selective compassion" causes great suffering. Empathy. Small word. Huge meaning. I believe Trixie was born "different" because she had a mission on this earth—to teach us about the enormity of that tiny word.

Now perhaps her mission is to greet new souls as they transition beyond the veil. There is no doubt she would be the very first at the gate, anxiously waiting to lavish endless kisses. She would especially smother toes with her smooches. One friend surmised it was because she knew her own little paws were designed more oddly than others.

Trixie was grace and joy in a tiny twisted body. She was hope and the beat of my heart. It is so broken without her, and the world is so much darker without her vibrant light. Trixie was a fighter and beat the odds all her life. But she lost her last battle, laid her head on my heart, and quietly took a final breath.

I knew when death came she would go silently, even then trying to be such a good girl, never wanting to make a fuss. My arms and home and soul are so very empty without her. My sorrow is profound. Now all that's left to embrace are memories.

And photographs.

I'll miss you always, little Doodle. The most pure and gentle soul I've ever been blessed to hold. I felt sad at times when she watched other dogs romp and play in ways she couldn't.

Now run like the wind forever precious angel. And rest on a cloud. We will meet again someday, over the rainbow.

Sweat Dreams, my beloved Trixie…

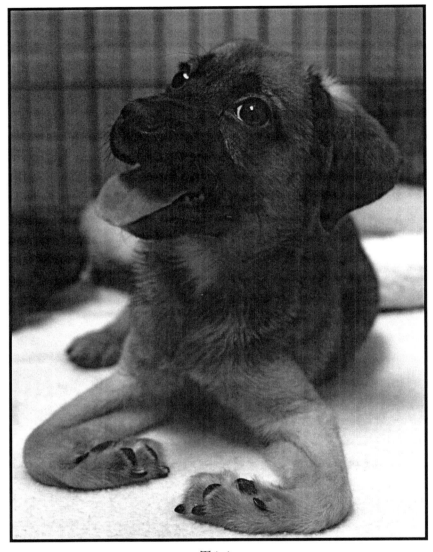

Trixie

Photo Credit: Carol Guzy

TRIXIE'S PLACEMENT POEM

Native American Prayer

The Sacred Hoop, the Circle of Life is complete
On this day as we return you to Earth Mother.

From Dust to Dust, Ashes to Ashes
We know the cycle, but we grieve your crossing.
Our grief is the love & memories you left with us.

You taught us to be responsible and sensitive to all life
And so we reflect on your teachings
And each perceives these through their window of understanding.

As we return your body, we release your spirit
That you may return to our creator to begin the circle anew.

Join your friends, you are whole again with no pain or imperfections.

We give thanks to your caregivers and say "Well Done"
Your works reflect your love, respect and commitment.

Your earthly journey is now complete and we say "Farewell Friend"

You will be missed, for as long as you dwell in the hearts you leave behind,
You will never die.

Amen, Aho

MY MENTOR, MY FRIEND
Sylvia Silvetti Havlish

December 31, 1974. Thirty-seven years ago. It should have been a New Year's Eve like so many others in my life. We were having a small gathering of friends in our small row house in Allentown, Pennsylvania. I was twenty-five years old and had just completed my Master's Degree in Counseling the preceding spring. Norm and I had been married for three years, I was employed as a guidance counselor at a local high school, and we were enjoying life and looking forward to welcoming in a new year with special friends.

Several of those friends were people I had met while in my graduate school program during the last three years. As the conversation progressed that evening, the topic turned to one of our most respected and popular professors. I'll call him "Dr. R" for his family's privacy. We were "singing his praises" as a great teacher and mentor. We were agreeing that he brought something very special to our counseling education…a caring, personal relationship with each of us. He was tough on us and challenged our thinking at every turn. But he did it with grace and élan. He was only thirty-five years old.

We had asked him to try and attend this little soiree and celebrate with us. As the clock started to near the midnight mark, several of us decided to call him and wish him the best new year ever. We felt that he had given us so much that we wanted to let him know just how special he was to us. We were going to have a group "shout" of

"Happy New Year" when he answered the phone. I dialed.

The phone was quickly picked up, and I expected to hear his "southern drawl" on the other end. However, instead, I heard the voice of one of our other professors...notably Dr. R's best friend on the faculty. His voice was somber.

"Sylvia, I'm sorry, but he died today at five p.m. I'm with the family, and I'll make sure to talk with you and the others at a later time. But I must tell you that today, he took his own life."

"He took his own life." I dropped the phone and screamed. It couldn't possibly be true. Not him. Not now. We were hugging each other and sobbing. I announced in some strange voice that the party was over and they should all go home. None of us could make any sense of this news. My husband told me later that I was running up and down our stairway and "muttering" like a "mad" woman. I don't remember doing that. I do remember that I didn't sleep at all and kept trying to make sense of a senseless loss of life.

The next day I insisted that my husband drive us ninety miles away to my best friend's home so that I could tell her in person. She attended all my classes with me, and I knew that she also had a very special place in her heart for him. I guess I thought that together we might be able to come up with some valid reason for him to take this action. Instead, we cried together, felt sick together, and made our husbands miserable right along with us. It was a horrible start to the new year.

Because his family was in the south, there were no local services. No way for us who loved him and respected him to have any closure at all. We had left the university the semester before this tragedy, and he was there. Now he was not there. In fact, we could not find him anywhere. We were left with so many unanswered questions.

It took me months to remember that I couldn't pick up the phone in my office and call him for advice when I encountered a counseling problem. I started to dial several times, and then the realization would hit me with a resounding thud. I remembered him telling us during one of our classes that counseling people after they had experienced the suicide of a close family member or friend was one of the most difficult sessions to have. Now the only counselor I wanted to talk with was him. He told us to never lose hope. He promised we would be able to find hope when we needed it.

I was eventually told that he had left a letter for us in his office. I was told that I could go there and read it. I could not make myself go to that office. I could not go there and see his office either empty or now filled with his "replacement." I forced one of my friends to go and then tell me about it. Hearing the "reasons" didn't give me the closure or peace I thought I would have. There was still a gaping hole in my heart and a searing hurt.

But then about one year after his death, I attended a convention for school counselors in Pennsylvania. And as if he orchestrated the "chance meetings" himself, about fifteen or so of us...the former students of this incredible teacher...found each other at a "welcome reception" the first night. As we would recognize each other, the very first thing we said was the question of "did you know about...?" The more wine and cocktails we consumed, the more determined we were to have our own "memorial service" in the courtyard that night! And we did.

I think he would have loved it! We sat in a circle...just like we did in his "Group Processes" classroom. We raised our glasses to this fine young man who imparted so much wisdom to us and sent us on our way to counsel people throughout the ages. We laughed, we cried, we remembered. He will never be forgotten. I think of him so many times as I counsel people now for the thirty-seventh year in a row. You were a Star, Dr. R. You will always be a Shining Star to me!

Sylvia Silvetti Havlish
March, 2012

CPSIA information can be obtained at www.ICGtesting.com
Printed in the USA
LVOW081013021012

301153LV00004B/2/P